CASE STUDIES IN EDUCATION:
A COMMONWEALTH VIEW

Coping with HIV/AIDS in Education

Case Studies of Kenya and Tanzania

Magdallen N. Juma Ph.D

Commonwealth Secretariat

Published by:
Commonwealth Secretariat
Marlborough House
Pall Mall
London SW1Y 5HX
United Kingdom

Further copies may be purchased from:
Publications Unit
Commonwealth Secretariat
Telephone: +44 (0)20 7747 6342
Facsimile: +44 (0)20 7839 9081
Web site: http//www. thecommonwealth.org

ISBN 0-85092-667-X

Price: £5.99

Printed by Formara Ltd

Contents

Acknowledgements

Thanks to the Commonwealth Secretariat's Education Department for the grant which made it possible for this study to be undertaken in Kenya and Tanzania.

The author is also grateful to Dr Katabaro of the University of Dar-es-Salaam and his research assistants for having co-ordinated the Tanzania case study.

Special thanks and appreciation to Mrs Jennifer Kere and Wasike, research assistants on the project. Jennifer did a wonderful job in Bondo District interviewing HIV/AIDS victims, schoolchildren, teachers, fishermen and officials from non-governmental organisations.

Finally, recognition and appreciation to my secretary Mrs Maria Nyawade for typing the report and to www.lawafrica.com for scanning photographs into the original printed version of the study.

General Introduction to the Series

Education systems are increasingly making changes in response to a rising tide of new expectations about the role of education in human development. Education is seen as a critical requirement for individuals to fulfil their potential, for communities to make positive changes in quality of life and for societies to improve their economic competitiveness. This rediscovery of education, as the key to human development, stems partly from the need to address growing inequalities within countries and between countries in an era of globalisation. The global era is characterised by rapid advances in technology and expansion of knowledge. It is therefore not unreasonable for political leaders to view education as a way of dealing with the opportunities and problems that stem from globalisation. In response, important changes are now taking place in the field of education. These changes concern opening up educational opportunities to all citizens, developing more flexible and responsive programmes, improving the relevance and quality of education content, and enhancing the organisation and management of education systems. Many countries are making progress in these areas of concern, but there is an urgent need to share success stories and lessons learned from these efforts so that they can be replicated where possible.

There is a new emphasis on partnership as a key guiding principle governing the ways in which countries work with international bodies, non-governmental organisations and the private sector, in the field of education. There is also a new realisation that countries have the main responsibility to provide appropriate education and training opportunities for all their citizens. This requires leadership and commitment as well as a wide range of budgetary and other resources, but many countries cannot achieve this by themselves. Partnership then becomes critical for involving NGOs, external agencies and the private sector in successful design and implementation of plans.

Partnership has always been one of the cardinal principles through which the Commonwealth operates as a voluntary association of countries sharing a common set of values and beliefs. In this regard the Commonwealth's work in education has a strong tradition of learning from each other. This new series on Case Studies in Education is the latest vehicle through which the Education Department continues to promote valuable exchange of experiences and good practice in the field of education. It is a series of key papers dealing mainly with innovations and challenges in education. The emphasis is on dissemination of the innovation or challenge in a timely and brief manner, but also in a focused way that provides description as well as analysis. This will make the case studies useful for those wishing to replicate the innovation or to have a better understanding of how a challenge can be tackled. It is the hope of the Commonwealth Secretariat that these case studies will be of benefit to countries, agencies and organisations within the Commonwealth and beyond. The series therefore marks an important Commonwealth contribution to the international partnership for advancing education and human development.

— useful

Abbreviations and Acronyms

AIDS	Acquired Immune Deficiency Syndrome
AMREF	African Medical and Research Foundation
APS	AIDS Programme Secretariat
CBO	Community Based Organisation
DASCO	District AIDS/STD Co-ordination
DC	District Commissioner
DHMTS	District Health Management Team
DIAC	District Inter-Sectoral AIDS Committee
DMOH	District Medical Officer of Health
FGD	Focus Group Discussion
FLE	Family Life Education
GOK	Government of Kenya
HAPAC	HIV/AIDS Prevention and Care
HIV	Human Immunodeficiency Virus
HSRP	Health Sector Reform Programme
IEC	Information, Education and Communication
KIE	Kenya Institute of Education
KREAR	Kagera Regional Education Annual Report
MOE	Ministry of Education
MOEC	Ministry of Education and Culture
MOH	Ministry of Health
MTP	Medium Term Plan
NACP	National AIDS Control Programme
NASCOP	National AIDS and STD Control Programme
NGO	Non-Governmental Organisation
NTC	National Task Force
PWA	People Living With AIDS
STD	Sexually Transmitted Disease

STI	Sexually Transmitted Infection
TIE	Tanzania Institute of Education
TOT	Trainer of Trainers
TRCS	Tanzania Red Cross Society
TSC	Teachers Service Commission
UNESCO	United Nations Educational, Scientific and Cultural Organisation
UNICEF	United Nations Children's Fund
VCT	Voluntary Counselling and Testing
WEC	Ward Education Co-ordinator
WHO	World Health Organisation

Executive Summary

The overall purpose of these case studies was to assess the impact of HIV/AIDS on education in selected districts of Kenya and Tanzania, and to review the various mechanisms in place in the affected communities to address the impact and challenges in education.

The study approach adopted in Kenya was a case study of Bondo District and some Nairobi city slums, while in Tanzania the study was conducted in Bukoba and Muleba districts in the north-west of the country on the shores of Lake Victoria. The case study approach was believed to provide thorough and in-depth information. It arises from the distinctive need to understand the complex social phenomena involved in the spread of and response to the HIV/AIDS pandemic. The districts covered by the case study were among the areas with the highest rates of HIV/AIDS infection.

The data collection techniques adopted for the case studies included a documentary review covering a variety of sources varying from media reports, research reports, workshop and conference reports, teaching materials, circulars, posters and leaflets. There were also Focus Group Discussions (FGDs), unstructured interview schedules, questionnaires and checklists.

A wide range of stakeholders were selected from all the sampled districts; they included teachers, NGO staff and education officers, as well as community leaders. A number of government and NGO officers involved in HIV/AIDS prevention programmes at the national level were also interviewed.

Data were analysed quantitatively and qualitatively. Quantitative data were computed into means and tabulated for interpretation, while qualitative data were analysed by identifying themes and trends, and categorised for interpretation and analysis.

From the analysis, it is clear that almost everyone in the communities studied had heard about the HIV virus and AIDS, although the problem appears to be one of assessing how widespread the menace is and its overall impact. There appears, however, to be some ambivalence about the severity of HIV/AIDS; the general tendency of many people in the communities surveyed is not to admit the seriousness of the HIV/AIDS menace. They perceive it as a common problem in their day-to-day lives which has taken its toll among children, young people and the middle-aged as well as the elderly. Some people still believe that HIV/AIDS is someone's creation and that treatment for it is being deliberately withheld in an attempt to reduce the population.

On the basis of the research method adopted by the case studies, determining the mortality rate with sufficient supportive evidence was quite difficult. This was partly due to a lack of concrete information regarding HIV/AIDS cases because of the lack of openness about the menace. It was also difficult to verify mortality rates from the local district hospital records. Through the FGDs and interviews, it was clear that the mortality rate of HIV/AIDS related cases is high. Some children infected at birth did not live long enough to attend school. There are cases of children being enrolled in school only to drop out in order to earn money to support their families and help with health care expenses for their sick relatives.

At the national level, especially in Kenya, there is some evidence of increased mortality as reflected in the recent national census the overall results of which showed a national decrease in the projected population. The case studies also revealed that the HIV/AIDS pandemic seems to be the most single important health challenge that Kenya and Tanzania, like other parts of the developing world, are facing. HIV/AIDS is a major health problem that has the potential to reverse the significant gains made in life expectancy and infant mortality.

The disease was said to be transmitted in various ways which included the sharing of sharp instruments, such as needles, during injections or ear piercing, and attending to HIV/AIDS patients, especially washing their bodies which have sores, as well as negligence in blood transfusion. The major cause, however, was identified as unprotected sexual intercourse.

The overall goal of the governments of Kenya and Tanzania is to slow down the progression of the HIV/AIDS epidemic, eventually bringing it to a halt, and to respond adequately to the consequences of the epidemic. To realise such goals, both governments have solicited funds from bilateral and multilateral donors, and increased their own funding. HIV/AIDS programmes have been launched which have focused on aspects such as management, information, education and communication, clinical services, counselling and mitigation of socio-economic impacts, epidemiology, surveillance, research and blood testing.

Although the programmes reflect a genuine effort to combat the spread of the pandemic, the response in the two countries was slow and took root after the disease had already had far-reaching and devastating effects. Generally, the programmes have not worked synergetically, with most of them being sporadic and patchy. Lack of political will in combating the pandemic is manifest at all levels of the political leadership, especially in Kenya.

To cope with HIV/AIDS at the community level, it was noted that there have been intensive sensitisation campaigns, especially in the urban areas, to warn the public about the HIV/AIDS problem. This has been done through public meetings convened by local leaders and churches that give warnings about the dangers of the disease, as well as providing counselling services. Hospitals and clinics use antenatal visits to make mothers aware of the dangers of the pandemic. On the whole, the sensitisation campaigns appear effective among the adult population although more still has to be done to change people's attitudes and behaviour.

Households use a variety of strategies to cope with the economic shock of a prime-age adult death. The most commonly applied strategy is drawing on family savings or selling assets. The ownership of land, livestock, bicycles and radios is quite widespread in rural settings. Many households that suffer an adult's death sell some of the durable goods as part of their coping strategy.

The death of a parent or another adult in the household quite often affects the nutritional status of surviving children by reducing household income and food expenditure. Such nutritional reduction impedes intellectual development and a person's long-run productivity. The effects of a prime-age death also lead to a fall in school enrolment among children in the household due to the reduction in the ability of families to pay for schooling; raising the demand for children's labour; and children being withdrawn from school to work outside the home, help with chores and farming, or care for an ailing family member.

From the communities studied, it is clear that they are experiencing a tremendous social strain in coping with large numbers of HIV/AIDS orphans. At the family level, there is already an increased burden and stress on extended family structures. Many grandparents and relatives are caring for young children and many go without the basic amenities. Many of the problems children experience at the household and community levels contribute to considerable absenteeism from school and dropout rates.

At the school level, it is clear from the case studies that pupils are well aware of the causes and dangers of HIV/AIDS. They learn of the problem from a variety of sources, including the media and the school. The HIV/AIDS education programme, especially in Kenya, appears quite weak. Despite the lack of a formalised approach in teaching about HIV/AIDS, schools in different regions have attempted various ways of imparting AIDS education, including specific programmes tailored towards the disease, and poems and drama.

Schools also try to cope with HIV/AIDS through material support to those affected, especially in cases of death, by contributing to funerals by way of donations and the provision of labour.

AIDS orphans generally have problems in coping with the numerous school levies, which in the end exclude them from school participation, although some schools give a special remission to such children. In the urban areas, there is a growing phenomenon of rehabilitation centres for children in need of special protection.

HIV/AIDS has an obvious effect on the management of teachers, especially their personal interactions with their peers, pupils and job retention. Many sick teachers, especially in the rural areas, take little official leave, as they fear rumours of stigmatisation and problems of redeployment or replacement. Consequently, some schools are generally understaffed due to the problem of sick teachers. This absenteeism is an important contributory factor to overcrowding in many schools.

1. Background

Introduction

The HIV/AIDS epidemic has left no part of the world untouched. The problem is worldwide, although the greatest concentration of HIV infections and AIDS related deaths is in developing countries. Several countries in sub-Saharan Africa, together with countries in south and south-east Asia, account between them for 89 per cent of HIV infections. Of the 16.3 million AIDS-related deaths which have already occurred, 13.7 million were in sub-Saharan Africa and 1.1 million in south and south-east Asia. By the end of 1999, an estimated 23.3 million people in the countries of sub-Saharan Africa, including over one million children, were living with HIV/AIDS. AIDS is said to have become the leading cause of mortality in the region, accounting in 1998 for 1.8 million deaths, compared with one million deaths from malaria (UNESCO, 2000).

Across the continent of Africa, and in several other affected areas, AIDS is already taking a devastating toll in human suffering and death. It is causing untold physical, psychological and emotional suffering. It is carrying off the most productive members of society, those in the 15–49 age range. It is disrupting social systems, exacerbating poverty, reducing productivity, wiping out hard-worn human capacity, and reversing development gains. Although it has only begun to scythe its way into many communities and economies, its ravages are increasing rapidly (World Bank, 1999).

In Kenya, it is estimated that over 1.5 million people have died of HIV/AIDS since the epidemic was first reported in 1984. In 1999 alone, about 200,000 people were estimated to have died of HIV/AIDS. By June this year, the number of infected cases was said to have risen to 2 million, of whom around 600,000 are children. The growing number of AIDS

1

orphans has imposed a heavy burden on families and communities and on the Government's ability to respond to the needs of these children. The realisation that the country is losing about 500 of its people daily to HIV/AIDS has led the Government to declare the pandemic a 'national disaster'. Around 75 per cent of HIV-positive Kenyans live in the rural areas and the majority are young people aged between 15–39 years. HIV/AIDS has been reported in every district of the country (Okeyo, 2000). Between 40–70 per cent of patients in medical wards in major public hospitals suffer from AIDS-related illnesses. AIDS has also caused a resurgence of many diseases that had been considerably reduced.

The AIDS pandemic in Tanzania was first reported around 1983. Given its long incubation period, AIDS might have been in the country much earlier awaiting diagnosis and confirmation. There is little doubt that this has had an effect on the spread of the HIV infection, especially during the initial stages of the pandemic (Katabaro, 1996).

Since 1983, the HIV infection rate spread and the number of full-blown HIV/AIDS cases have increased tremendously. For example, it took only one year from the first case being reported in the Kagera region, for all the regions of Tanzania to report full-blown cases of HIV/AIDS. Furthermore, the exponential rate of increase evidenced by the number of cases within a short period of diagnosing the first case and subsequent cases, shows clearly that the disease had gained roots before it was clinically confirmed. For instance in 1983 there were three cases in Kagera region, followed by 103, 322 and 847 cases in the years 1985, 1986 and 1987 respectively. This trend is evident in all other regions of Tanzania. Available statistics suggest a similar pattern in other countries. For example, in 1983 about 187,000 cases were reported by WHO as compared to over 500,000 cases in 1992. By 1993 the figure was estimated by WHO to be 2.5 million (Kaijage, 1993).

The impact of the tragic scenario of HIV/AIDS is already being felt in every aspect of socio-economic life including formal education.

2

Insufficient research has been done to support an objective assessment of the extent of the impact, but various indicators tend to show it as considerable. HIV/AIDS is affecting pupils, teachers, parents and communities, organisations and management, the curriculum as well as resources.

There are various ways in which HIV/AIDS impacts on the formal school system. At the macro-level, AIDS will have the long-term effect of there being fewer pupils to educate. This will be as a result of significantly shrinking populations. In the coming couple of years the Kenyan and Tanzanian populations in some parts of these countries will be smaller than they would otherwise have been. The losses will be because of large increases in adult and child mortality, a lower fertility rate and some reduction in the number of births due to the premature deaths of women in their child-bearing years. This demographic development will considerably reduce the number of pupils of primary school age.

Although hard evidence of the negative impact of HIV/AIDS on school enrolment and attendance has yet to come to the surface, there are indications that some districts and regions of Kenya and Tanzania have been experiencing stagnation in enrolment and, at times, a decline in the numbers of pupils attending primary schools. This has been happening at a time when the number of school-aged children is increasing, when the number of children not attending school is already very large and when primary school facilities are not being used to the full. This decline in school participation rates is attributed mostly to poverty and to parental disillusionment with the low quality of education that schools provide, as well as lack of employment. Although comprehensive studies have still to be conducted, it seems likely that some of the decline in school participation in some districts and regions is also due to AIDS, and to the impact this is having on poverty and levels of employment. In addition, children from AIDS-infected families have to generate income for family support or are needed to care either for the sick or for young siblings.

3

The impact of HIV/AIDS on teachers has been a subject of public interest and debate in recent months. Although hard figures of infection among teachers, like other public employees, are hard to come by, a recent Ministry of Education statement in Kenya reported over 30 per cent of teacher deaths in Nyanza as being due to HIV/AIDS. The report prompted the Teachers Service Commission (TSC) to direct a nationwide HIV/AIDS test of all teachers. The directive was roundly condemned, forcing the TSC to withdraw the mandatory tests. While one cannot attribute all teacher deaths in Nyanza to AIDS, 30 per cent is undoubt-edly high in terms of costs to the profession and to the Government. HIV/AIDS would also affect the deployment of teachers, especially those infected and posted to remote areas, because they have to seek medical treatment in town. The infection is likely to affect their productivity since they are traumatised and stressed.

In terms of resources, HIV/AIDS victims deprived of the breadwinner in the households are left without resources to pay school fees and to meet many of the educational needs of their children. Within households, a large proportion of the greatly reduced resources may be devoted to treat-ment at the expense of educational costs of children, especially girls. Furthermore, with communities weakened through poverty, hunger and sickness, they will be unable to participate in self-help activities for schools.

Coping with HIV/AIDS

With the catastrophic effects of HIV/AIDS now being experienced world-wide, many countries have implemented intervention strategies to cope with the pandemic. Studies are beginning to show that specific interven-tions using voluntary counselling and testing (VCT), condom social marketing, peer education and treatment of sexually transmitted infections (STIs) can change behaviour patterns and reduce the risk of HIV infections. More importantly, it has been shown that the synergistic effect of combining these interventions reduces the risks even further (World Bank, 2000).

In Kenya, although the first case of HIV/AIDS was diagnosed in 1984, the epidemic was not considered a serious problem until the late 1980s when the Government launched a comprehensive five-year Medium Term Plan (MTP) in which the AIDS Programme Secretariat (APS) was established to control HIV/AIDS under the guidance of the National HIV/AIDS Committee. The Medium Term Plan focused on the prevention of HIV infection by screening blood, promoting safer sexual practices and early diagnosis of Sexually Transmitted Diseases (STDs). It also focused on developing a national public awareness, publishing guidelines on testing and counselling and training health care workers in the management of HIV/AIDS patients. Also recommended was the need to decentralise HIV/AIDS activities and greater advocacy (National AIDS Control Council, 2000).

In 1991 the Government developed a Second Medium Term Plan (MTP-II), in which it sought to mobilise other sectors in the fight against HIV/AIDS. Non-governmental and private sector groups were included as partners in the national response, although the responsibility for managing Kenya's response remained within the Ministry of Health. In 1992, the AIDS Programme Secretariat (APS) was elevated to the status of a National HIV/AIDS Control Programme (NACP). The main strategies pursued by the NACP included the prevention of sexual transmission, prevention of mother-to-child transmission and epidemiological surveillance. In recognition of the central role that STDs play in enhancing the risk of HIV transmission, the hitherto separate STD programme was merged with NACP in 1993 to become the National AIDS and STD Control Programme (NASCOP).

Although the MTP-II was ambitious in its strategies, it was inadequately funded; hence, the prospects of major social and economic projections stated in the plan did not generate an equivalent response on the ground. Many religious organisations also opposed efforts to introduce sex education in schools, and condom promotion was and still is opposed by some influential religious leaders. A variety of legal, ethical and cultural issues related to prevention and the well being of HIV/AIDS-affected families still remain (National AIDS Control Council, 2000).

The implementation of programme activities resulted in the recognition of AIDS as having a negative impact on various sectors of development. The Government therefore adopted a multisectoral approach in the fight against AIDS, resulting in the integration of AIDS in the seventh National Development Plan and the district development plans.

The National AIDS Control Programme in Tanzania, as elsewhere, was launched to spearhead the national efforts to fight the HIV/AIDS pandemic. In pursuing this goal the programme, which was first conceived as a National Task Force (NTF) in 1987, established four technical units charged with different aspects of the pandemic. One of these units was the Information, Education and Communication (IEC) Unit. It was charged with the dissemination of vital information, statistics and facts about HIV/AIDS and related complexities, as well as with educating people about various aspects of HIV/AIDS infections (Katabaro, 1996).

In the absence of a cure and vaccine, the option of AIDS education was the most viable alternative. It was anticipated that education would help to control THE further spread of HIV infections and develop positive attitudes and perceptions of the victims of AIDS among the general population. The assumption was that awareness would lead to informal decisions across the range of behavioural patterns and attitudes (WHO, 1990). Evaluative studies conducted in Tanzania and elsewhere have confirmed this assumption. However, they have also indicated some elements concurring with those studies showing that little or no change has taken place at all in some sections of the population (Muhondwa et al., 1991; Ndeki et al., 1994).

AIDS education in Tanzania started seriously in the late 1980s through mass media campaigns. These activities characterised the first national Medium Term Plan in the fight against AIDS. More emphasis came to light during the MTP-II after 1991, when AIDS education was introduced in workplaces, particularly in urban areas, and in schools (Katabaro, 1996).

Community members and, in particular, religious groups had mixed feelings about AIDS education. This was mainly due to the fact that most of the content of this programme was not clear to parents and religious leaders and was, therefore, not acceptable. It appeared to these groups that the content was mainly focused on sex education, which had been previously rejected by the same groups (Sawaya et al., 1995). This atmosphere indicated that not only was the community denied participation in the formulation of the AIDS education package, but also that the objectives were not made clear to the entire community. The programme has still to be approved for circulation to the schools in the country.

It was therefore apparent that lack of proper planning was beginning to affect these programmes in the realisation of their objectives. As has often been emphasised, such interventions need to consider the local social and economic environments. In particular, taking stock of some cultural and social aspects of the communities before embarking on programmes of this nature is essential. More serious is the limited involvement of the communities (Kaijage, 1993).

At the sectoral level, each sector is expected to respond to the HIV/AIDS scourge in every possible manner. In the absence of curative drugs and prophylactic vaccines, the only viable way of dealing with the pandemic is through developing appropriate standards of behaviour with information being translated into types of behaviour that promote healthy communities.

In this and other AIDS-related areas, education is perceived as being the most powerful instrument to mitigate the impact. Education can mitigate the impact of HIV/AIDS and its consequences through its potential, first and foremost, to reduce the likelihood of infection by developing values and attitudes that prevent premature, casual or socially unacceptable sex and sexual experimentation. Second, education strengthens the capacity of those who experience HIV/AIDS, whether in themselves or in their families, to cope with the problem. Third, in the event of death through AIDS, education assists the student or teacher in coping with grief and loss by helping in the reorganisation of life in the aftermath and, finally, in a more generic way, education plays a key role in establishing conditions that render the transmission of HIV/AIDS less likely, namely, conditions such as poverty reduction, personal empowerment and gender equality (UNESCO, 2000).

The community attempting to intervene to mitigate the impact of HIV/AIDS through education has responsibility for the incorporation of HIV/AIDS education into the curriculum with a view to bringing about behavioural change. The Ministry of Education in Kenya, for example, recognises the importance of education and the promotion of right attitudes towards HIV/AIDS. Consequently, efforts have been made by the Kenya Institute of Education (KIE) to revise the school curriculum to provide some opportunity to address the attitudes and behaviour of young people through the inclusion of life skills and reproductive health. As a result of the multi-dimensional nature of HIV/AIDS, the KIE has adopted the integration approach. In this approach, HIV/AIDS is not given the status of a separate subject. It is instead treated as a cross-cutting issue which is addressed in all subject areas and which could be examinable as part of those subjects. The programme which is supposed to have been introduced in the schools at the beginning of September 2000 faces, among others, the following bottlenecks:

• The government cannot meet the cost of publications.

• Teachers are not ready to handle the subject. In view of their vulnerability, they have to be inducted before they are ready to disseminate materials to pupils/students.

In Tanzania, AIDS education in schools was approved in 1993 when, in practice, a subject on AIDS was allocated time on the school timetable. This was followed by a short in-service training course for teachers, especially in the Kagera region, on how to teach the new and sensitive subject. The training was made possible by the Tanzania Red Cross Society (TRCS). The TRCS met all the training costs including teachers' allowances and other training materials. In collaboration with the Tanzania Institute of Education (TIE) of the Ministry of Education and Culture (MOEC) and other NGOs, they prepared the syllabus, and pupils' and teachers' handbooks. The production of multiple copies was delayed due to financial constraints at the MOE (Sawaya et al., 1995). More training sessions were, however, offered by the MOE through the generous funding of UICE. These sessions were limited to only a few teachers from each school. A major constraint of AIDS education at the primary school level has been a lack of teaching/learning materials and inadequate training for sufficient numbers of teachers (Katabaro, 1996).

The situation was even worse at the secondary school level where the teaching of AIDS education did not start due to the lack of trained teachers and teaching materials. In the Kagera region and in those areas where NGOs dealing with HIV/AIDS were active, there were visits and guest speakers who gave talks and showed films about AIDS. A few secondary schools in Bukoba district also received instructions and discussions offered by one NGO, the Médicins du Monde (Katabaro, 1996).

It is understood that a major policy objective in education is to use the sector's potential to slow down the rate of new HIV/AIDS infections, help

9

its infected members to cope, and support those among them who have been bereaved by the scourge. Part of the sector's response in this area has been the introduction of life-skills programmes. These aim to influence health and social behaviour by seeking to develop student ability in five key psycho-social areas: self-awareness, interpersonal relationships, decision-making and problem-solving, creative and critical thinking, and coping with emotions and stress. Other countries in the eastern and southern Africa region have also endeavoured, with mixed success, to integrate programmes of this nature into their school curricula. Common problems with this approach include lack of teacher knowledge and confidence, tendencies to gloss over sensitive sexuality issues, the perception that because it is not examined the area is not important, and inadequate efforts to mobilise the support of parents and other key stakeholders (Gachuhi, 1999).

However, among the better-documented programmes and interventions, especially those which rely on peer education and peer counselling, are some in the non-formal education sub-sector. Working outside the formal school setting with various youth clubs and religious groups is more productive because participants take part freely without any coercion. Their interest and commitment are reasonably well assured from the out-set. The self-selection factor, however, means that the positive outcomes of anti-AIDS clubs and similar groups in schools might not extend beyond the actual membership, although in such situations the participants experience more pressure from their peers and from the school authorities to take part in such activities.

At the community level, religious and community leaders are normally expected to play a leading role in advocacy. They are perceived to have a greater impact on influencing behavioural change. Particular emphasis is placed on the population sub-groups at greatest risk, such as youth in and out of school, women, members of the armed forces, populations residing in special geographical locations such as slums, commercial sex workers, long distance drivers and others (National Aids Control Council, 2000).

Purpose and Objectives of the Study

The overall purpose of this study was to assess the impact of HIV/AIDS on education in selected districts of Kenya and Tanzania, and the various coping mechanisms in place in the affected communities to address the impact and challenges for education. More specifically, the study aimed at examining:

- The impact of HIV/AIDS in terms of pupil enrolment, participation, drop-out and completion;

- The impact on teacher management in terms of deployment, professional and personal interaction with infected teachers, their peers and pupils, and treatment and care;

- Coping mechanisms at the school level, for example, the effect of family life education, youth clubs and management of teachers;

- Coping mechanisms at the household and community levels.

Importance of the Study

As already stated, this study focuses on the impact of HIV/AIDS on education and on how education is coping with it. In view of the fact that neither cure nor vaccine are likely to be available to those affected and to those potentially affected in the near future, methods for prevention of the further spread of HIV/AIDS and better care of the affected, as well as coping with the aftermath of its calamity, remain the major priority in coping with the scourge. Moreover, effective prevention interventions are a function of good and proper planning through identifying the needs and priorities of the beneficiaries, understanding the environment within which the programmes operate, and the adoption of better methods and approaches.

The findings of the study will be of particular assistance to current and potential NGOs in the planning and execution of health education programmes on HIV/AIDS. They can also help government policy-makers in policy formulation, monitoring and the co-ordination of such programmes in the country. It was also hoped that programme implementers such as school teachers, health workers and social workers would find the study valuable in adopting better approaches for the execution of their programmes.

The study is also a useful contribution to the existing body of knowledge about the impact of HIV/AIDS on education and the coping mechanisms being adopted in response to the scourge. The study is also informative for the general public among whom, to a great extent, there still lingers a terrible misconception that HIV/AIDS only affects other people and not themselves. For some time now HIV/AIDS has remained an epidemic of stigmas, denials, rationalisation and ignorance.

The Study Approach

The approach adopted is a case study of Bondo District and some slums in Nairobi city in Kenya. The case study approach is believed to provide thorough and in-depth information. It arises from the distinctive need to understand the complex social phenomena involved in the spread and response to the HIV/AIDS pandemic. Nyanza Province and Nairobi city, from which the case studies have been selected, are among the areas with the highest rates of HIV/AIDS infection, estimated to be around 25–40 per cent of the population.

The samples from the two districts included district education officers, health officers in the health centres in the areas of study, NGO staff, head teachers and teachers, youth groups, and pupils from Standards VII and VIII from each selected school. It also included community leaders as well as religious leaders. The selection of these respondents was purposive in order to obtain the required information. The identified categories of the sample were considered to have the required information about the impact of HIV/AIDS and the coping mechanisms adopted by the schools and communities.

The data collection techniques adopted for the study included a documentary review covering a variety of sources varying from media reports, research reports, workshop and conference reports, teaching materials, circulars, posters and leaflets. There were also focus group discussions, unstructured interview schedules, questionnaires and checklists.

Interviews were held with 6 head teachers, 30 teachers, NGO staff, education officers and health officers in the selected districts, while FGDs were conducted with selected community leaders. Questionnaires were administered to Standard VII and VIII pupils in three sampled schools in Bondo District and three sampled schools in Nairobi city. In all, 230 pupils responded to the questionnaires.

Data were analysed quantitatively and qualitatively. Quantitative data were computed into means and tabulated for interpretation while qualitative data was analysed by identifying themes and trends and categorising them for interpretation and analysis.

In Tanzania, the study was conducted in Bukoba and Muleba districts in the northwest, on the shores of Lake Victoria. In each district only one ward was chosen for the study. Selection of the wards was influenced by the severity of the HIV/AIDS pandemic; the most and least affected wards were avoided to eliminate extreme results.

The sample of the study included two district education officials of the two districts and two health officials from the health centres in the same area of study. The sample also included six school head teachers and 240 students (from grades VI and VII). Eight opinion leaders of different backgrounds and two Ward Education Co-ordinators were also included in the sample. Staff members from NGOs within the two districts were also involved. Both purposive and convenient sampling techniques were adopted in order to obtain the required information.

The study adopted a variety of data collection techniques, including unstructured in-depth interview schedules, questionnaires, observations (non-participatory and participatory), focus group discussions and documentary review.

Interview schedules were used to collect information from adult participants while the questionnaire method collected data from pupils. Observations and FGDs were used with different groups of participants to assess the impact of HIV/AIDS on attitudes and people's opinions. The techniques used helped generate both quantitative and qualitative information about the impact of HIV/AIDS on education in the study areas.

Quantitative data were computed into percentages, and tabulated for interpretations. Qualitative data were analysed by identifying the themes, patterns and categories of information that helped the interpretation of data.

2. The Kenya Case Study

The Impact of HIV/AIDS

HIV/AIDS at the National Level

At the national level, there is some evidence of increased mortality as shown by the recent census. In Kenya, the overall results of the last census, carried out after an interval of 10 years, showed a national decrease in the projected population. Kenya's population projected in 1993 for the year 2000 was approximately 32 million in the absence of a major catastrophe like HIV/AIDS. The recent census population data put Kenya's population at 28.9 million, more than three million below the expected figure. This was reported to have been a big shock for the Kenya Government, to the extent that there were reports of concern in government circles leading to attempts to manipulate the census data after the disclosure, overturning the common belief that the country's population had hit the 30 million mark (Odiwuor, 2000).

HIV/AIDS in Schools

From the analysis, it was clear that almost everyone in the communities studied had heard about the HIV virus and AIDS; the problem was to assess how widespread the menace is and its overall impact. As captured in one FGD: 'they have some good knowledge about what HIV/AIDS is, but it is often referred to as a third party. Even those directly affected do not accept the fact all that quickly'. The headteacher of one of the schools in the rural district of Bondo denied the presence of HIV/AIDS within the school and the community.

Schoolteachers in the same school, however, described how the community was experiencing HIV/AIDS-related cases. The problem apparently stems from the fact that no post mortems are done on local deaths which AMMP do not reach the district hospital. It was stated: 'every other day there is at least one burial in the area neighbouring the school. Within the proxi-

verbal autopsies   15

mity of the school, in less than five kilometres radius of the school, there are up to four or five funerals in a week.'

In many instances, reported cases of pupils infected by HIV/AIDS in schools were generally said to be quite few. However, reported cases of teachers who are either HIV-positive or have died were common in both rural and urban districts covered by this study. Teachers mentioned colleagues who had died on their staff or in neighbouring schools, although during the discussions it was pointed out that since medical records regarding the illnesses of individual teachers were, on the whole, confidential, it was difficult to establish with certainty whether or not their colleagues had suffered from HIV or died of AIDS.

The problem of establishing the nature of illnesses also applies to parents and community members who had suffered or had died of HIV/AIDS. As was explained in one of the FGDs:

Information on how HIV/AIDS affects parents and members of the community is generally difficult to ascertain, although talk either of parents suffering or those who have already succumbed to the disease is quite common in the area. Four of the teachers listed a total of ten parents who they are sure have succumbed to the disease. It was also stated that deaths of community members and parents have been on the increase, being the main factor contributing to some of the school drop-outs experienced by the school in the last few years.

The sexual activity of male schoolteachers with pupils is one of the factors that is facilitating the spread of HIV/AIDS, and is therefore a problem of increasing concern to parents and administrative officials. More and more cases are being reported of male schoolteachers using their official authority, their age and experience to take sexual advantage of schoolgirls who are often ignorant of the sexual and reproductive process and practice. In many parts of Kenya, schoolteachers are often placed in schools outside their own home districts, and are frequently transferred in the course of their careers. Because they move frequently without their spouses, they constitute a high-risk group for the introduction and transmission of HIV and other sexually transmitted diseases.

HIV/AIDS in the Community

On the whole there appears to be some ambivalence about the severity of HIV/AIDS in most of the communities studied. There is a general tendency by many people in the communities surveyed not to actualise or admit the seriousness of the HIV/AIDS menace. They tend not to perceive it as a common problem in their day-to-day lives, although it has taken its toll among children, young people and the middle-aged as well as the old. Some in the communities still believe that HIV/AIDS is someone's creation and that its treatment is being deliberately withheld to extensively reduce their population.

It is, however, apparent that in the townships where HIV/AIDS has taken on a more dangerous form, many of the respondents appreciate its seriousness, although they do not know their own status because they do not go for an HIV test. As the FGDs confirmed, such a dilemma exposes more people in the areas to HIV/AIDS through their risky behaviour.

Using the research method adopted by this study, finding sufficient supportive evidence to determine the mortality rate was quite difficult. This was partly due to a lack of concrete information regarding HIV/AIDS cases, as has been pointed out above, as well as lack of openness on the part of some respondents about the HIV/AIDS menace. It was also difficult to verify mortality rates with the local district hospital records. From the general discussions with the teachers and through the FGDs, however, it seems that mortality rates of HIV/AIDS-related cases are high. Children have been infected at birth and have therefore not lived to attend school. From the FGDs, information was garnered that a significant number of children die before they can be enrolled in school. Consequently, investing in education is perceived to be no longer useful because of the increase in child mortality. The various reasons for the high mortality rate included the lack of immunisation, especially in rural areas. There were some cases of children being enrolled in school only to drop out in order to earn money to support their families and help with health care expenses for their ill relatives.

The discussions ascertained that the major impact of HIV/AIDS in the communities has been the creation of poverty within the districts. This view was expressed by some of the officials from the various ministries, such as planning, who are able to assess the poverty in all parts of their respective districts. There are key factors in the synergetic relationship whereby an increase in poverty level is seen to correspond with an increase in the severity of the HIV/AIDS menace. The HIV/AIDS pandemic seems to be the most single important health challenge that Kenya and Tanzania, as indeed other parts of the developing world, have faced in their recent history. It is the only health problem that has the potential to reverse the significant gains made in life expectancy and infant mortality. The HIV/AIDS pandemic has, therefore, become much more than just a health problem as it embraces economic, social and cultural dimensions. Kenya and Tanzania are suffering expensive losses of trained manpower, while the cultural, legal and socio-economic consequences of the disease are aspects with which the countries have as yet to cope (Odiwuor, 2000).

As regards how the various communities came to learn about the existence of HIV/AIDS, sources of information were quite varied. In one community around Lake Victoria the most fascinating source was a relative of a member of the FGD who used to visit Kenya; in 1984 the relative informed the community of 'a terrible disease which was killing people in Uganda through raha (enjoyment). Later on in 1985, through the radio, messages were sent out about a horrible disease that had come and was going to kill many people. It was later termed UKIMWI (AIDS)'. In practically all the FGDs, there was a consensus that they began learning about HIV/AIDS in the late 1980s and still continue to do so. Sources of information included the radio, churches, barazas (local meetings), TV, offices and people discussing about the disease in public places, like markets.

The disease was said to be transmitted in various ways, including the sharing of sharp instruments such as needles during injections or piercing ears, but unprotected sexual intercourse was identified as the major cause, together with attending to HIV/AIDS patients, especially washing their bodies which have sores, as well as negligence in blood transfusion. A certain kind of behaviour was, however, said to be a major contributor to the spread of HIV/AIDS. In the urban settings, for example, 'drunkards', particularly arising from the many illegal brews that are traded in the slums, were thought to be responsible, as well as single mothers who exposed themselves to prostitution. A member of the FGD stated: 'single mothers . . . wanataftita pesa kwa njia zote (look for money in all ways) and the single men who also happen to be working with them'.

In the slum areas of towns, cases of rape were also said to be on the increase recently, especially with the growing state of insecurity in many parts of Nairobi. These cases of sexual assault involved the targeting of young girls often because of the belief that this group was AIDS free. Apart from this, there was also a belief that if infected men had sex with young girls, they would be cured of the disease.

In some parts of the study areas, it was admitted in the FGDs that most people in the community were not aware of the HIV/AIDS situation, and this was of particular concern to the community leaders. Such communities still saw HIV/AIDS as a social and cultural problem. There were many who held to traditional beliefs like viewing the disease as a curse, or 'chira' among the Wajaluo of Western Kenya, and therefore sought healing from

African herbalists or spiritual healers on discovering that they were HIV-positive. In some of the FGDs, because our respondents were not ready to point a finger at suspected HIV cases or dead people, their illnesses or deaths were attributed to cultural beliefs and taboos. Thus members of the community would say, 'so and so did not observe certain rituals when her husband died, in the case of a dying widow, or that the disease was the result of a curse that the dying man had brought to himself by being seen naked by his daughter'. They also talked about professional wife inheritors (people who habitually inherit wives) whom members of the FGDs said would be intimate with a mother, daughter and even grandmother depending on the demand and payment. This practice was said to be causing considerable havoc in some of the communities studied.

One activity said to be a major contributor of HIV/AIDS in the Bondo district of the study was fishing along the beaches of Lake Victoria. At the fishing beaches, there were activities that contributed to the spread of the disease. It was said that beaches have leaders whose responsibility it was to oversee activities on the beach. Those who wish to buy fish from the beach have to be registered with the beach leader before they are allowed to do so. Women are the ones normally sent to the beach to purchase the fish from the fishermen and carry them inland to the markets.

Most of the fishing is done at night and early dawn, so that by 9.00 a.m. all the fish is already sold. A woman who needs fish has one of two options. She can either spend the night at the beach waiting for the fishermen to come in with their catch, or she can make the journey to the beach very early in the morning before all the fish has been sold. Normally, it is better to spend the night at the beach. Beaches usually have makeshift houses and eating places. It is the responsibility of the beach leader to assign these women to some men who 'take care' of them whenever they come to purchase fish. Any woman who refuses to be assigned a caretaker is never allowed to do business on that beach, and in most cases is chased off the beach. The beach leaders claim that if a woman does not want to have a caretaker, then it means she has intentions of prostituting herself on the beach with all the fishermen (Odiwuor, 2000). This information was strongly corroborated during the FGDs.

Since fishing is mostly carried out at night, the fishermen have the rest of the day to idle around with lots of their money from the fish sales. The excess money in the hands of the fishermen also attracts young girls and boys of school age. These girls and boys try to generate income on the beaches. 'The beach leader syndrome' often leads young people into prostitution for financial gain and it is therefore a major contributory factor to the spread of HIV/AIDS in the district (Odiwuor, 2000).

According to the FGDs, the possession of money greatly contributes to the spread of the disease. Workers in the rural areas were said to be exposed to high risks of contracting HIV/AIDS 'because they have money and therefore socially interact with a wider variety of men and women with possibilities of indulging in activities that enhance the spread of the disease'. The disease was, however, said to be too expensive to cope with. As indicated in one of the FGDs:

> The people cannot afford proper and recommended diets for the sick relatives, they cannot afford to pay hospital bills or buy the recommended medicines.

This, they insisted, hastened the death of many AIDS victims in the area. Apart from the expenditure on drugs and medication, treatment of HIV/AIDS patients has further drained a lot of resources from the already impoverished community. It was emphasised 'we have seen with our own eyes what this disease is capable of doing to an individual and, more so, to the family earnings/savings'.

Coping Responses at the National Level

The overall goal of the Kenyan Government is to slow down the progression of the HIV/AIDS epidemic, eventually bringing it to a halt, and to respond adequately to the consequences of the epidemic. To realise this goal, the Government solicited the input of the World Health Organisation (WHO) and bilateral and multilateral donors in order to finance AIDS programmes. This enabled the government to allocate funding for AIDS programmes in the Ministry of Health (MOH). Funding has increased tremendously over the years, and provides for both national and district level implementations. In the 1996/97 financial year the government further invested in health by securing a World Bank loan of US$40 million for the control of Sexually Transmitted Infections (STIs). Recognising the importance of mobilising local resources, the Government has actively promoted community participation, involvement of NGOs, Community Based Organisations (CBOs), the private sector, philanthropic organisations and individuals (Government of Kenya and Unicef, 1998).

As part of the efforts to reduce the transmission of HIV and mitigate the impact of AIDS, the government's policy is to promote and strengthen non-institutional care of people with HIV/AIDS. There is also a policy shift regarding breastfeeding of infants in view of the risks of transmission of HIV from mother to child through breast milk. *other health risks ?? Substitute ??*

HIV/AIDS Programmes

The implementation of HIV/AIDS programmes in Kenya follows the steps outlined in the Policy Framework Paper of 1996–98 and the Kenya Health Policy Framework of 1994 which emphasised, among other things, decentralisation in decision-making and delegation of authority to plan and implement HIV/AIDS prevention and control activities at district level.

At the national level, the NASCOP has four major programme components, which include:

- programme management;

- information, education and communication (IEC);

- clinical services, counselling and mitigation of socio-economic impact;

- epidemiology, surveillance, research and blood safety.

Programme Management

Based on the decentralised system and in keeping with the Health Sector Reform Programme (HSRP), districts and provinces receive direct allocation of funds from the Treasury to plan, implement, monitor and evaluate HIV/AIDS programme interventions. NASCOP provides technical support to strengthen the institutional capacity of districts, NGOs, CBOs and the private sector. It also co-ordinates inputs from donor agencies, government ministries or departments and other stakeholders. At the district level, implementation is under the leadership of the District Health Management Teams (DHMTs), headed by the District Medical Officer of Health (DMOH), supported by a District AIDS/STD Co-ordinator (DASCO) who is a member of the DHMT. In order to enhance inter-sectoral collaboration, a District Inter-sectoral AIDS Committee (DIAC), chaired by the District Commissioner (DC), is in place in every district, with membership drawn from government ministries, NGOs, the private sector and community leaders.

Each of the four components of NASCOP is backed by a technical sub-committee which plays an advisory role in the management of AIDS programmes. As a division within the MOH's Department of Promotive and Preventive Health Services, NASCOP is headed by a programme manager and provides leadership in the collective response to the epidemic. The main focus areas are the prevention of sexual transmission, prevention of transmission through blood and blood products, mitigation of the socio-economic impact of HIV/AIDS, epidemiological surveillance, co-ordination of research and finally the management and co-ordination of the multisectoral AIDS Control Programme.

Information, Education and Communication

The implementation of IEC programmes centres around the use of the mass media, interpersonal communication and advocacy. The main thrust of IEC is awareness creation and enhancement of knowledge for behaviour change in the prevention and care of HIV/AIDS. The primary objectives of IEC are to enhance positive advocacy on STI prevention, enhance capacity-building at all levels, reduce STIs through the adoption of safer sexual behaviour, enhance health care seeking behaviour in target groups, especially for the treatment of STDs and reduce the transmission of STIs through practices other than sex.

Clinical Services, Counselling and Mitigation of the Socio-Economic Impact of AIDS

This is a programme component encompassing the clinical care of persons with STDs, counselling support for people living with AIDS (PWAs) and the reduction of the socio-economic impact of AIDS on individuals, families and communities. The treatment of STDs is an important control of HIV infection and includes the syndromic management of STDs and adequate training of health workers. Drugs for STD management are procured and distributed to health facilities through a 'Drug Kit System' involving the private sector and NGOs.

The magnitude of the HIV/AIDS epidemic and its consequences on the health care system have made counselling and the provision of social support important elements of care. Despite the limitations, the training of counsellors has been undertaken by the Government, NGOs and support groups for people living with AIDS. However, there has been a shortage of counsellors to meet the increasing demand (Government of Kenya and Unicef, 1998).

Epidemiology, Surveillance, Research and Blood Safety

Epidemiological surveillance and research is designed to provide information on the trends of the epidemic to policy-makers and programme planners so that they can understand the magnitude of the problem and formulate interventions. This information is generated through reported AIDS cases and surveillance. NASCOP has endeavoured to issue all health facilities with a special form for reporting AIDS cases, followed by the training of health workers on how to use the form. The government has also ensured safe blood supply through a process which involves the identification of low risk donors, screening of all transfused blood for HIV victims and other patients.

Impact of HIV/AIDS National Programmes

Although the above programmes to combat the spread of HIV/AIDS reflect some genuine efforts to stem the spread of the pandemic and rehabilitate people living with AIDS, the response was, on the whole, slow in coming and took root after the disease had had far-reaching and devastating effects on the population. Generally, the programmes have not worked synergetically, with most of them remaining sporadic and patchy rather than evolving more comprehensively. They have also tended to lack political will in expressing a national commitment and providing overall leadership to the nation in response to the pandemic. There has been a lack of effective responses characterised by strong political commitment from the community leadership up to the highest political leadership, as demonstrated by erratic pronouncements from leaders at all levels of society regarding HIV/AIDS.

Coping Responses at the Community Level

Anti-HIV/AIDS Campaign

To cope with the HIV/AIDS pandemic within the communities studied during the FGDs, it was noted that there have been intensive sensitisation campaigns, especially in the urban areas, to warn the public about the HIV/AIDS problem. This has been done through public meetings convened by local leaders and churches which give warnings about the dangers of the disease as well as providing counselling services. There are also community leaders who are involved in preventive activities such as trainers of trainers in advocacy campaigns. Hospitals and clinics use antenatal visits to expose mothers to dangers of the pandemic. In such gatherings and campaigns considerable emphasis is placed on avoiding unprotected sex and the dangers of immorality.

On the whole, the sensitisation campaigns appear effective among the adult populations although more still has to be done to change people's attitudes and behaviour. As the following summary of the views of an FGD indicates:

> Of late sensitisation campaigns have tried to take the message to the people's doors and have been trying to wrestle with deep seated beliefs about the disease. They insisted that many of those who have been infected still maintain that the disease comes as a result of witchcraft. Furthermore, many of the youths have frustrated campaign efforts and need more attention and other talks due to the influence of the media, films and videos. It was the feeling of the group that more effort, especially with the use of films in the community can change their attitudes towards the disease. Some comments coming from the youth about the disease which need to be seriously addressed include:
>
> • many say that HIV/AIDS is just like malaria and other diseases;
>
> • HIV/AIDS is contracted by sheer accident;
>
> • there is the belief that eating meats that are not commonly eaten, as well as certain foodstuffs, are cures for HIV/AIDS.

Consequently, it is quite common for many young men to be seen moving to and continuing to live with sick women whose HIV/AIDS symptoms

youth views (margin annotation)

are quite visible. Overall, therefore, the campaigns may have increased HIV/AIDS awareness, but they have not had much impact on attitudes and change of behaviour. As was also noted:

Results have not been seen because people are still suffering and dying in large numbers. Only a few follow instructions given by experts. Physical appearances are quite deceptive as they lead one to think that his/her sexual partner is healthy and therefore there is no need to use condoms.

At the family level, parents revealed that they often try to be frank with their children as much as possible on matters relating to HIV/AIDS. In many cases, especially in the urban settings, parents tend to talk to their children with a lot of confidence and seem to have no problems or fears, since the children are perceived to be already aware of the dangers of the disease through the media, especially radio, television and magazines, or through discussions with their teachers at school. Although in some cases children tend to resent what they consider to be interference with their privacy, they on the whole listen attentively although they are also categorical that parents are not in a position to gauge the effectiveness of their communication as they cannot always monitor what their children do while at school or when they meet their peers outside the home.

With regard to organisations involved in the campaigns to sensitise the communities about HIV/AIDS, there is the unfortunate situation that most of them are concentrated in the urban centres, especially in the slum areas. Many of the organisations have very patchy activities in the rural districts. Most of the organisations are either NGOs or have links with organised religion. Government institutions seem not to be heavily involved in the anti-HIV/AIDS campaigns. The most frequently mentioned organisations in the Mukuru Slum of Nairobi included AMREF, which started campaigns and training of TOTs in 1990 but terminated the training in 1992/93, and the Catholic Church, related to the Mukuru Promotion Centre, which trains TOTs and community health workers as well as carrying out door-to-door campaigns. They also train TOTs in Family Life Education (FLE) for two weeks to promote its activities among the residents. Doctors without borders (Médicins sans Frontières) personnel also brought films in 1998 which were shown to the residents for one week. The City Council health personnel are also involved in campaigns and sensitisation programmes. Locally based organisations such as the Kayaba Unity Development Group, a local initiative, have not been quite as successful due to the lack of finances as well as lack of more informed leadership to spearhead the campaign.

In the Baba Dogo Slum of Nairobi some key organisations, including the Crescent Medical Aid, as well as Action-Aid (Kenya) and World Vision are working in the community. The work of one particular church, the Redeemed Gospel Church, happens to be the most visible in the community. especially in the provision of medicine and mounting seminars for local people.

Coping by Households

Emotional Stress and Medical Expenses

From the outset, it needs to be pointed out that in addition to its devastating impact on infected individuals, HIV/AIDS hurts all those who are linked to them by bonds of kinship, economic dependency or affection. The grief suffered by survivors, and the possible lasting psychological damage especially to young children who lose a parent, are potentially the most damaging consequences of the epidemic, although they are the most difficult to measure. Above all, the death of a prime-age adult is obviously a tragedy for any household.

Death causes emotional stress

Akinyi (not her real name) died during my in-depth interview with her husband. It was a very sad experience.

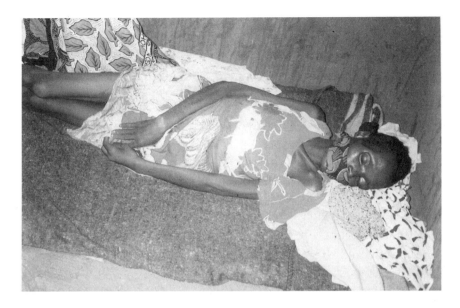

Akinyi was 25 years old

Akinyi's husband

This man has 16 wives, and Akinyi was the last wife. During the interviews, he sadly expressed his situation as follows:

> I made a mistake in life by marrying many wives and having many girl friends. My women have been dying one by one. I am also going to die.

Survivors must contend not only with profound emotional loss but also with medical and funeral expenses, plus loss of income and services that a prime-age adult typically provides. The direct impact of a death consists of the medical costs prior to death and the costs of the funeral.

In the FGDs, it was clear that people diagnosed with HIV/AIDS were somewhat more likely to seek medical care than people who died from other causes, and they were more likely to incur out-of-pocket medical expenses. Moreover, household medical expenses tended to be much higher for HIV/AIDS than for other causes of death. On the average, households spent nearly 50 per cent more on funerals than they did on medical care and this particular situation is quite common, especially in the western parts of the country. The relative amounts spent on medical care and funerals, of course vary across communities even within a given district.

The Economic Response
Households use a variety of strategies to cope with the economic shock of a prime-age adult death. The most commonly applied strategy is depleting savings or selling of assets. The ownership of land, livestock, bicycles and radios are much more widespread in the rural settings. Evidence from Bondo suggests that many households which suffer an adult's death sell some durable goods as part of their coping strategy. Evidence of households depleting savings from a traditional savings and credit association to cope with an adult death was quite common. Depleting savings usually has the consequence of reducing participation and membership in such associations. It was, however, also established that new organisations are

often set up to help cope with costs of AIDS deaths. It was found that besides traditional savings and mutual assistance associations, residents of many villages launched associations specifically to help families affected by an AIDS death. Most of these associations were launched and operated by women; and many of them had regular meetings at which members made contributions in cash or in kind.

Nutritional Status of Children

The impact of adult death on childhood nutrition is likely to vary according to many factors, not least of which is the nutritional status of children in the overall population. Little information is, however, known on how adult death affects child nutrition. What is clear is that childhood nutrition is potentially one of the most severe and lasting consequences of a prime-age adult death. The death of a parent or other adult may lower the nutritional status of surviving children because household income and

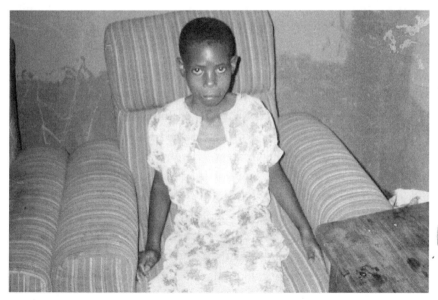

This orphaned child is HIV-positive

31

food expenditure may be reduced and less attention may be given to child rearing. Because childhood malnutrition can impede intellectual development and thus reduce a person's long-term productivity, improving childhood nutrition has been an important development goal in both Kenya and Tanzania. Available research seems to show that among the poorer households in the Kagera region, for example, stunting (very low height for age) among children under 5 is indeed substantially higher for orphans (51 per cent) than for children whose parents are both alive (39 per cent) (Lwihula, 1990).

Reduced Support for Schooling

Besides increasing childhood malnutrition, a prime-age adult's death in a household reduces school enrolment. This lack of schooling, exacerbated by inadequate nutrition, makes it particularly difficult for child survivors of a prime-age adult's death to escape poverty. The effects of a prime-age adult's death on children in the household include: reducing the ability of families to pay for schooling; increasing the demand for children's labour; and reducing the expected returns to adults of investments in children's schooling.

As already noted above, charges in income and expenditure that occur before and after a death tend to reduce the ability of families to pay school fees and other education costs. Children are also withdrawn from school to work outside the home, help with chores and farming, or care for an ailing family member. In addition, in areas where prime-age adult mortality is high, parents are generally less willing to invest in their children's schooling, either because they fear that the children will not live long enough to realise the higher earnings schooling promises, or because the parents themselves do not expect to live long enough to benefit from their children's future earnings. Similarly, relatives who take in orphans are generally less willing than the parents would have been to invest in the children's schooling. For all these reasons, children who have lost one or both parents have lower enrolment rates than those whose parents are alive.

HIV/AIDS Orphans in the Community

Research evidence on the state of HIV/AIDS orphans in Kenya is still quite scanty and it was not possible for this study to focus on that particular aspect. Anecdotal evidence, however, shows that many children who have lost their parents through the disease are seriously traumatised. Without financial assistance, for instance, these children's chances of obtaining education are severely reduced. The psychological trauma some of these orphans undergo tends to instill a feeling of despair about the future. They have to strive for survival by engaging in child labour. It is also clear that financial support alone does not answer the children's emotional needs, which often leads to poor concentration, tantrums and hysteria.

Some studies show that orphaned children have the following choices: staying in their parents' houses to look after themselves; living with grandparents, uncles, aunts and other relatives; and living in some form of institutional care (Caldwell et al., 1989). In 1992, in Kenya, UICE estimated that the number of children to be orphaned by HIV/AIDS would reach one million in the next decade.

From this study, it is apparent that the communities which were observed are experiencing a tremendous social strain in trying to cope with large numbers of HIV/AIDS orphans. At the family level, there is already an increased burden and stress on the extended family structures. Many grandparents are caring for young children. The FGDs revealed that there are some families which are headed by children as young as 10 or 12 years old. Many of these children go without adequate health care and schooling.

Although the samples for this study were relatively small so that possible generalisations from them are limited, it was apparent that the school drop-out rate was generally high, and that most of those who dropped out of school lacked school fees, uniforms, textbooks and other school requirements. Following the death of parents many children leave school and girls are said to resort to prostitution. Many of the urban centres have in recent years witnessed a growing number of street children. In the villages there are also orphaned girls who assume the role of mothers in the homes to provide essential services to their siblings. In this desperate role as mothers they are liable to unwanted pregnancies or premature marriages or engage in commercial sex that exposes them to a higher risk of HIV/AIDS infection. The orphans left under the custody of relatives fare no better as they are also deprived of basic amenities such as food, clothing, shelter and medical care.

It is quite common for HIV/AIDS orphans to be dispossessed of their late parents' property. Loss of property ranges from the slaughter of the only milk cows during the funeral festivities to the grabbing of immovable property such as shops and land. These orphans are mostly vulnerable to unscrupulous relatives, especially if they happen to be girls whose rights over land ownership are often limited under traditional customs. The problem of property ownership emanates from the fact that there are serious superstitious beliefs regarding the writing of wills which is believed to be signalling death to oneself. Consequently, many HIV/AIDS patients, even those on the verge of death, refuse to write wills in favour of their children, making it difficult for them to bequeath property.

The FGDs also showed that quite often close relatives of HIV/AIDS patients tend to distance themselves from their sick kinsmen and women, leaving their care to the children whatever their age. Children in such circumstances absent themselves or drop out of school in a desperate bid to assist their ailing parents. This is often due to fear and misguided beliefs regarding the disease. Such relatives tend to treat the sick as pariahs and leave all the responsibility to the helpless children who watch their parents suffer from a prolonged and undignified illness which subsequently kills them.

The experiences of the orphans are quite deplorable, especially the exploitative nature of some of the so-called carers. During the FGDs a number of distressing cases were narrated. There was, for example, the case of a twelve-year-old boy and his brother who was ten, who were left in the custody of an uncle together with their eight-year-old sister. The uncle hired them out to work as herdboys and a baby sitter, respectively, telling them that the money they would earn would be used towards paying the cost of their education. As it turned out, the money was used to educate his own children. The matter was reported to the headteacher and chairperson of the school committee of their former school, for possible intervention. There was no means of effective intervention and in the end the children abandoned their places of employment and travelled to Kisumu to seek new opportunities.

There was also the case of a Standard VI pupil whose parents worked in Kisumu. The father died first, followed by the mother in a period of less than three years. The boy was left to be taken care of by an elderly aunt near Bondo town. The boy, like other orphans who are taken care of by elderly relatives, found it difficult to meet the financial costs associated with schooling, which include school uniforms, books, writing materials and school levies. Pleas by the elderly aunt to the headteacher for consideration of the financial difficulties fell on deaf ears because he could not bend the rules . This led to the boy dropping out of school altogether. It was emphasised in the FGDs that there were many similar cases and that these had been inadequately addressed by primary schools in this area.

Coping Responses at the School Level

HIV/AIDS Awareness

The school remains a central place of learning and the only key institution which contacts many children, teenagers, their families and communities. In this regard, the school is quite important in having a systematic and long-term influence on attitude and behavioural change. This section reports on HIV/AIDS awareness and coping responses at the school level.

It focuses mainly on pupils and teachers.

The HIV/AIDS awareness level is likely to make the required impact to alleviate the situation. The spread of HIV/AIDS infection can be halted largely through awareness and the provision of resources to address it. Young people, in particular, are critical in this process since they are more receptive to new ideas, learn more quickly and are at the start of their sexual lives. It was therefore important in the study to assess how pupils perceive what HIV/AIDS is all about. It was also important to find out if they had been given information about how people become infected with HIV/AIDS, how it can be avoided and how they relate to the victims of the disease.

Pupils' Perceptions about the Most Serious Disease

In a questionnaire, Standard VII and VIII pupils were asked what they considered to be the most serious health problem which their country (Kenya) was facing. The respondents wrote down the diseases as they perceived them. Figure 1 shows how pupils in different schools viewed what

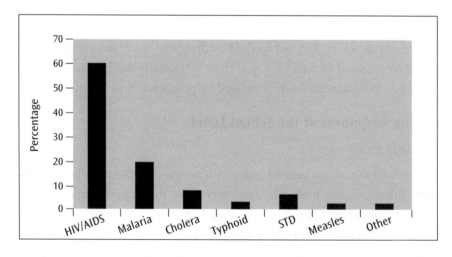

Figure 1. The most serious health problem in the country

they perceived to be the most serious health problems. In their responses 60.5 per cent indicated that HIV/AIDS is the most serious problem facing Kenya today. It was followed by malaria with 20.6 per cent, cholera with 5.5 per cent, typhoid and other diseases which were not specified. Most of the pupils, 96.9 per cent, had heard about the existence of HIV/AIDS. They were also aware how HIV/AIDS is caused. Among the commonly mentioned causes of HIV/AIDS were having sex with many people; having sex with persons who were HIV positive; blood transfusion; and use of needles and syringes.

Sources of HIV/AIDS Information

The most commonly cited source of information about HIV/AIDS was the radio (16.4 per cent), followed by newspapers (14.5 per cent), school (14 per cent), family/relatives (12.9 per cent), friends/schoolmates (10.8 per cent), clinics and hospitals (10.1 per cent), churches and others. Although we did not desegregate our data on the school settings, namely, rural and urban schools, it was apparent that pupils in the urban schools got much of their information on HIV/AIDS from newspapers and the

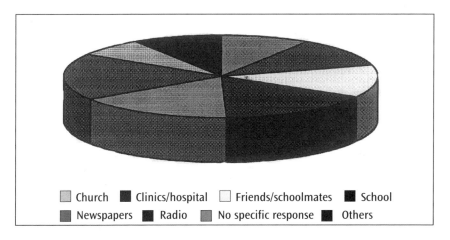

Figure 2. Sources of information about HIV/AIDS

37

radio. This is attributed to the fact that most of their parents could be working class, unlike parents in the rural schools. Many can afford to buy newspapers and listen to the radio, which often transmits information about HIV/AIDS as a deadly disease.

Schools in the urban settings also benefited from posters as mechanisms of transmitted information about HIV/AIDS. Posters and billboards, especially along major highways, have become major sources of spreading information about the disease. The problem is, however, that too often the same information is transmitted for too long to such an extent that people tend to disregard its existence regardless of the prominence of the information. There is, therefore, a need for dynamism in changing the information and styles of dissemination.

What is most amazing is that the school is not a leading source of information. It is also evident how little the church seems to be doing to propagate HIV/AIDS awareness to pupils in the communities studied. Other sources included information from youth organisations. These groups could enhance programme design with more credible messages and create a climate for social and peer support for responsible and preventive behaviour. There were also NGOs focusing on HIV/AIDS which visit schools and the surrounding communities. These NGOs are either involved in preventive or support activities and have first-hand experience of the disease and its impact; they can provide valuable assistance in the design and delivery of credible messages about HIV/AIDS.

HIV/AIDS Information in Schools – Family Life Education

As already noted, the school does not seem to be the main source of information about HIV/AIDS for children in the study on Kenya. It appears HIV/AIDS education has as yet to take root in the Kenyan education system. As shown in Figure 3, 50.4 per cent of the pupils heard about HIV/AIDS in Home Science, 15.4 per cent in Science, 19.6 per cent, in

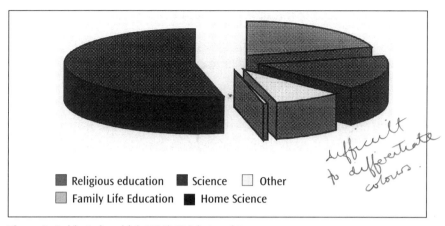

Religious education ■ Science □ Other *difficult to differentiate colours.*
Family Life Education ■ Home Science

Figure 3. Subjects in which HIV/AIDS is taught

Religious Education and a very negligible percentage in GHC, and have no information at all about Family Life Education.

The delay in introducing Family Life Education in schools in Kenya has been due to the controversy that has torn apart the various stakeholders over the subject within the Kenyan education system. This has tended to polarise parents, teachers, religious leaders and members of the communities. The issue has not been whether or not FLE should be taught, but how the teaching should be approached. One recommendation is that the MOE should ensure that there are specially trained educators to conduct school-based FLE programmes. This would add an important dimension to children's ongoing sexual learning. These programmes should be developmentally appropriate and should include such issues as self-esteem, family relationships, parenting, values, communication techniques and decision-making. The planning of the curricula should include all the stakeholders in education in order to respect the diversity of values and beliefs present in the country as well as the classroom and the community. A comprehensive FLE programme should, according to the National Guidelines (1991), have four main goals:

- To provide accurate information about human sexuality;

- To provide an opportunity for young people to develop and understand their values, attitudes and beliefs about sexuality;

- To help young people develop interpersonal skills.

- To help young people exercise responsibility regarding sexual relationships, including addressing abstinence, how to resist pressures to become prematurely involved in sexual intercourse, and encouraging the use of contraception and other sexual health measures.

Religious leaders in Kenya have been the leading opponents of FLE, arguing that it should be done with some sensitivity and by people of integrity. It must involve parents and religious leaders and have the aim of preparing young people for marriage and parenthood. Religious leaders consider it essential that children should be protected from exposure to all types of FLE that are immoral in context and intended to indoctrinate. They also insist that parents or other responsible persons in their lives are the right people to impart information to children about their developing sexuality.

The use of condoms also remains a very sensitive matter. There seems to be general agreement that it is not the task of religious leaders to promote condom use as a means of limiting the spread of HIV/AIDS infection. They stress that their policy of chastity before marriage and faithfulness within it should be adhered to. However, some religious leaders are now trying to bring about an informed responsible discussion on sexuality including the use of condoms, thus enabling individuals to make appropriate and responsible decisions. This shift has been as a result of religious leaders' acceptance that HIV/AIDS is not only a medical but also a moral epidemic for which they have no cure. Because of the devastating impact of HIV/AIDS even among the so-called 'Saved Christians', the Christian church is being compelled to take a fresh look at what it can do to fight the menace. Furthermore, the church is feeling the pressure to take action because secular institutions have failed to respond to the problem more effectively. The HIV/AIDS pandemic is being seen as a manifestation of the disintegration of traditional moral controls on behaviour which village life used to provide. It is also the consequence of rampant sexual freedom among teenagers which results in more and more schoolgirls dropping out of school because of pregnancy (Odiwuor, 2000).

HIV/AIDS Programmes in Schools

Despite lack of a formalised approach in teaching about HIV/AIDS, schools in different regions of the country have attempted various ways of imparting AIDS education. In Bondo District, for example, there is the Primary School Action for Better Health (PSABH) programme which tries to encourage pupils to talk about problems brought about by HIV/AIDS. Schools have also adopted a method whereby pupils in the upper grades are required to form groups to help in educating each other on matters relating to HIV/AIDS. Some pupils are taught communication skills to help present information on the disease. They compose poems about HIV/AIDS which are recited to peers, the entire school and the community. The poems focus on the devastating effects of the disease on both youth and adults, guarding against immoral behaviour and other ways in which the disease is transmitted, resorting to quack doctors for treatment and cautioning communities on traditions and beliefs such as wife inheritance and polygamy.

The Out of School Non-Formal Education (NFE) Programme on HIV/AIDS

The HIV/AIDS Community Communication Intervention of the HAPAC Project implemented by Ace Communications in Nyanza targets youth in and out of school, church-based youth groups, social welfare groups, women-led organisations and individuals in leadership positions.

The project is designed to provide information on HIV/AIDS that facilitates behaviour change through video shows and discussions.

The African Medical and Research Foundation (AMREF), through the Ministry of Education, has also sponsored teachers' workshops to educate drama and music teachers on how to organise meetings and plays for HIV/AIDS awareness for both pupils and the community. The drama and music festivals are organised for performances during the school days for pupils and for the general public during national occasions with the approval of the DEO. Some of the themes for the workshops are the effects of HIV/AIDS and how to live positively with the disease, abstinence and many others. Such workshops also focus on how teachers can effectively communicate HIV/AIDS messages to pupils, how teachers can share knowledge between themselves and health professionals. The workshops also focus on the use of choir and folklore in sending awareness messages especially on sexual behaviour, basic HIV/AIDS symptoms and the wasting away of victims.

Although the workshops also focus on such aspects as water, sanitation, nutrition, education and related matters, they demonstrate how HIV/AIDS is beginning to have a major place in the activities of the schools. The education system is planning its programmes on the disease with a clear perspective. Teachers have to devote part of their valuable time in fighting the HIV/AIDS disease. The classroom approach has to be much broader to include the community as well as being appropriate to the pupils. To be interesting to the two groups, the teaching approach has to be much more creative and in a language that is easily understood. HIV/AIDS is therefore giving the school the responsibility of being an advocate for family life education.

School Support for Funerals

Schools also try to cope with HIV/AIDS through material support to those affected especially in cases of death. In some of the rural areas involved in the study, within a short distance from the school there could be as many as three to six deaths in a week. This included, in some cases, deaths of teachers in the neighbourhood. In such a situation if a particular school was directly affected, all the schools in the community had to take at least three days off to attend and participate in the funeral arrangements. Male pupils, in particular, are organised to help in building temporary shades to accommodate guests who attend the funeral. Girls participate in fetching firewood and water for preparing meals for the guests. In the FGDs in Bondo, it was established that it is a custom for the community to feast at funerals.

In the case of a teacher's death, all pupils in the neighbourhood schools are required to donate some money towards the bereaved family to assist in buying food for the guests. Teachers are also expected to make their own contributions towards their bereaved colleague's family. Since so many deaths appear to happen each week, these arrangements become quite debilitating.

HIV/AIDS Orphans and Schooling

The deaths of parents affected schoolchildren in many ways. Pupils coming from homes where deaths had occurred had sporadic school attendance. Schools which usually have class enrolments of 45 to 50 pupils ended up having around 20 to 25 children on average attending school at different times, with more than 25 pupils being absent from class daily. Absenteeism, therefore, tends to seriously undermine the quality of instruction and the ability of teachers to cover the planned class teaching programme. Pupils, on their part, are not able to follow up the course content that was taught during their absence. Absenteeism here is occasioned largely by attendance at funerals and how the orphans cope with the situation in the absence of the prime-age adults. As captured in one of the FGDs:

Pupils have lost parents and other relatives. This has interrupted their going to school and negatively impacted on their getting basic needs, let alone school requirements. They start with irregular attendance and subsequently drop out or migrate to live with other relatives wherever they may be accepted. Such families disintegrate. Consequently, relatives acquire added responsibility if not an added one as in most cases they normally have children of their own to look after. Quite often some of them were living away from their ancestral home while their brothers and sisters were living at different places with different relatives and in many cases engaged in child labour.

Some specific examples of such children were as follows:

Consolate's 12-year-old sister was baby sitting for her aunt. Ochieng was living with his aunt (mother's sister). Aoko lived with her grandmother and Adhiambo with her aunt, as Perez, like Consolate, lived with an unemployed brother. They all said that life had changed for them as they were considered as extra loads in families they lived with. Due to school requirements, they could not afford such things like levies. They were therefore often out of school, sometimes just called back by teachers who sympathised. This meant that they lost a lot of learning time.

Maureen, in Standard V, and her two younger brothers live with their 58-year-old paternal uncle and his wife. Maureen's uncle said that the little money he gets is spent on food which has become very costly due to drought. He has no specific plans for the children's education, and spends on educational needs only when basic needs have been met. This means that most of the time the children stay at home due to unpaid levies and hardly have required textbooks and exercise books. The youngest brother is asthmatic and is often out of school due to his condition. The older boy was also sick and had been sent to their aunt to seek herbal medication. He had missed classes now the third day running.

15-year-old Peter is in Standard VIII and is the first born in the family of 5.

He is living with his mother's sister. Their last born who is in nursery lives elsewhere with his maternal grandmother. Two others are living with his father's brother. His sister lives with a cousin who is a teacher in a nearby secondary school. So he says 'my siblings are everywhere'. A cousin helps in paying for school requirements.

Kenneth is 16 years old and also in Standard VIII. He is living with a paternal grandmother. Two young sisters in Standards III and VII live with their aunt in Nakuru and Nairobi respectively. Although relatives are responsible for him, in most cases he does fishing in the evenings to get money to buy necessities including paying school levies. He says it has not been easy and concentrating on studies is quite hard.

A Case of a Child-headed Family

Onyango (not his real name) is 22 years old. He lost both parents two years ago. He is now the head of the family and has to take care of two brothers and one sister.

During the interview Onyango said the following about his situation:

My parents died, and left a four-month-old baby who also passed away after a few days. I had then to drop out of school to look after my brothers and sister. Life is very difficult for me. We had nothing left for us after the death of our parents, our chickens and pans were taken away by relatives. Nobody wanted to stay with us. We were branded HIV/AIDS children.

Although non-payment of school levies generally excludes most AIDS orphans from attending school, there were some schools that allowed such orphans to have fewer texts and exercise books than those expected from other children. They were also exempted from demands for school levy payment. They were given time, in some cases, to look for what was required without necessarily being sent away from school. This was strongly supported by responses in the pupils' questionnaires in which 42.2 per cent indicated that schools gave orphans remission to fee payments. Schools also gave some kind of counselling and this was supported by 24.1 per cent of the pupils.

Rehabilitation

Some form of institutionalisation of orphans is becoming a major feature of rehabilitation, especially in the urban areas. Many such centres have been set up in recent years. The most prominent is the Mukuru Promotion Centre, located in Mukuru slums in the industrial area of Nairobi. At present the centre runs four schools that are located in the slums neighbouring the main Mukuru slum. The schools are: Mukuru Centre, Kayaba Centre, Lunga Lunga Centre and St Catherine. The four centres are coordinated from the Mukuru Promotion Centre. They cater for children and youth from the slums as well as from the streets of Nairobi and other destitutes such as AIDS orphans, refugees and those displaced during ethnic clashes. The Kabiro initiative is situated within Kawangware slums of Nairobi and serves the people of Kawangware and Riruta slum areas.

HIV/AIDS orphans at Mukuru Promotion Centre, Nairoibi

Kibera – a rehabilitation institution in a slum area of Nairobi

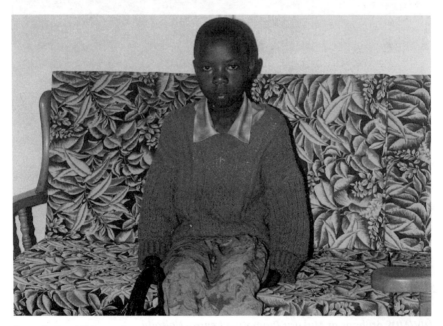

One of the children who came to the Centre

One young girl (see picture opposite) who came to the centre said:

I have no other relative in this world, so my mother told me this morning that if she dies I take my things and come here to stay. You will give me food and care for me. So I have come.

The formal schools serve primary-school-age children whose parents or relatives are unable to send them to government primary schools due to poverty. The management of the Mukuru and Kabiro initiatives have flexible policies on admission age while school uniform is not a requirement in Mukuru schools. The schools admit children who are sometimes a little over age and place them in academically appropriate classes following an internal assessment. The children are then progressively promoted. Because of this flexibility, the schools attract children who have dropped out at various classes and those who never had access to formal schooling. The most needy children in the initiatives are helped to find sponsors.

The projects also provide health services to all members of the community, particularly those from the surrounding slums. The Kabiro centre provides immunisation and growth monitoring for the under-fives, teaches FLE to the youth, provides family planning services and diagnostic services for minor illnesses and sells prescribed drugs from the community pharmacy. The projects provide counselling services to individuals and families, particularly those affected by HIV/AIDS. The Mukuru Centre provides shelter to children from very far off slums, street children whose parents cannot be immediately traced and other destitute children. All the children in Mukuru schools are provided with lunch while those who shelter there get supper and breakfast as well.

Both Mukuru and Kibiro centres have non-formal education programmes which focus on skills training for young people. Of the Mukuru centres, Kayaaba offers courses in carpentry and masonry in addition to formal schooling. The Kabiro Community Centre teaches tailoring and carpentry. Both centres offer counselling and FLE to the young people.

Pupils' Attitudes Towards HIV/AIDS Victims

At the school level, it was generally gratifying to learn that pupils have positive attitudes towards their fellow pupils who have been infected with HIV/AIDS. For example, in response to the statement that 'students infected with HIV/AIDS should not be allowed in school', 27.8 per cent indicated 'yes', while 58.7 per cent responded 'no' and 13.4 per cent indicated 'not sure'. With regard to the statement that 'HIV/AIDS victims should be shunned or avoided', 32.2 per cent said 'yes', 51.7 per cent indicated 'no', and 16.1 per cent were 'not sure'. As to whether people with HIV/AIDS should be isolated, 26.5 per cent said 'yes', 60.9 per cent said 'no', while 12.6 per cent were 'not sure', as shown in Table 1.

Table 1. Pupils' attitudes towards HIV/AIDS victims*

	Yes	No	Not sure	Total
Students infected with HIV/AIDS should not be allowed in school	27.8% (64)	58.7% (135)	13.4% (31)	100.0% (230)
HIV/AIDS victims should be shunned/avoided	32.2% (74)	51.7% (119)	16.1% (37)	100.0% (230)
People with HIV/AIDS should be isolated	26.5% (61)	60.9% (140)	12.6% (29)	100.0% (230)

*Figures in brackets indicate the number of respondents

Teacher Management

Deployment of Teachers who have Contracted HIV/AIDS

HIV/AIDS has an obvious effect on the management of teachers, especially of infected and ill teachers in terms of employees' rights to confidentiality and job retention. Professional and personal interaction between infected teachers, their peers and their pupils; employee treatment and care and the need to transfer infected teachers to areas of the country with better medical care, are issues that require particular attention. The staffing of schools in areas heavily affected by HIV/AIDS could also pose serious logistical problems (Shaeffer, 1993).

In the interviews with teachers in the sampled primary schools, many seemed to know of colleagues who were infected with or died of AIDS. In one of the schools, for example, they knew of two colleagues who had passed away as a result of HIV/AIDS-related sickness. They could not, however, ascertain the number of those who had died in neighbouring schools, although they cited four cases of some schools within their school zone who had succumbed to the disease. In another school it was stated by the teachers:

> This school has always been understaffed by at least two teachers at any given time. Last year when a teacher was intermittently sick, and during the last three months when he was hospitalised, the school had to adjust. Apart from distributing his subjects and considering the fact that the school was already understaffed even with the sick teacher, the teachers reorganised the timetable and deviated from covering the expected number of periods per subject per week. They worked on the number of periods which could be handled, e.g. instead of six sciences, they taught four.

They also donated money from their own pockets to help the teacher buy drugs and food. It was, however, still insufficient. This was besides giving him leave of absence locally without informing the employer as regulations require.

Teachers further claimed that victims were transferred from schools where powerful power brokers were stakeholders and could easily influence the DEO to do so.

In another school, where teachers more or less echoed similar sentiments it was noted:

> The teachers stated that replacement of teachers used to be very easy before.

Replacement was often effected as soon as the headteacher made the author-ities aware of the problem. It has, however, become very difficult these days. They stated that while it appears a bit easy in the upper classes as teachers teach different subjects, things are a bit complicated in the lower primary since at this level, teachers have been allocated classes (one teacher per class). It is a little difficult to share out these responsibilities unless new teachers come to the school. There are situations in which some classes have to be dissolved or merged.

In the discussion with the teachers a good number of issues came to the surface regarding HIV/AIDS infected teachers, some of which are identi-fied in the quotations above. First and foremost, sick teachers, especially in the rural areas, hardly took official sick leave, particularly if such sick leave was on a routine basis. They feared rumours of stigmatisation and of their illnesses being associated with HIV/AIDS. Such association would seriously discredit them. This situation puts the schools concerned which are understaffed in a very difficult situation. Most headteachers in the study tended to blame the TSC over its policy of replacing teachers which was said to be very slow and cumbersome. Furthermore, it was pointed out that the TSC found it much easier and convenient to terminate the con-tracts of sickly teachers than offer them sick leave and better medical benefits to seek proper treatment in their posts. This situation seems to have been aggravated with staff retrenchment advocated under the SAPs.

Although there were cases where the TSC offered sick teachers the chance to transfer to a school near their homes, for reasons already indicated most teachers found it impossible and inappropriate to ask for permission to stay away from work on health grounds. They worry that taking sick days could cost them their job. This is why such permission is sought locally between the headteacher and the affected teacher. However, if such sick leave becomes so regular that it is noticeable, the education office in most cases chooses to terminate the sick teacher's employment. Such a move often means additional financial problems for the teacher and leads to the inability to buy the needed medication.

Teachers' Absenteeism and the Quality of Instruction

Most schools, especially in the rural district covered by the study, were said to be understaffed. This is because of the problems of sickly teachers and the procedure the headteacher has to follow to get a teacher replaced, which is generally quite cumbersome. The chain of hierarchy before some officer finally gives authority for a replacement involves the headteacher reporting the matter to the zonal inspector, who in turn requests the divisional level up to the DEO, whose turn is to communicate with the TSC. Sometimes such bureaucracy takes as long as one year before the affected school gets a replacement.

In the meantime, the affected teacher is sick and his/her lessons are severely affected. Although schools do their best to reorganise teaching schedules, many of the lessons of affected teachers go uncovered during their absence as the remaining few teachers become more and more overburdened. In many cases a new teacher is not brought in until after the ailing teacher has died. In this way many pupils suffer as the quality of primary education continues to deteriorate in the country. In some areas due to the absenteeism of HIV/AIDS infected teachers which leads to classes being combined as a way of coping with the situation, classrooms become so overcrowded as to make it difficult for any meaningful teaching and learning to take place.

3. The Tanzania Case Study

The Impact of HIV/AIDS

The Problem of Orphanhood in Tanzania

The findings of this study confirmed the fact that orphanhood is becoming a serious problem in the education service. One of the most difficult conditions created by AIDS is the increase in the number of children who are orphaned due to AIDS. The Kagera Regional Education Annual Report (KREAR) of 1996 shows that there were 46,350 orphans out of 199,450 pupils (aged 7–17) enrolled in primary schools. Orphans constituted 23 per cent of the total pupil population. The projection based on these figures gives a figure of 805,000 orphaned pupils out of the national primary school population of 3,500,000. There are variations in the statistics of orphans reported by different sources. The figure reported by NACP (1997) of 100,000 orphans varies substantially from that reported by the Regional Social Welfare Department in Kagera region.

A systematic evaluation of school conditions in one affected rural district indicates that the number of orphans was 16,175 (27.6 per cent) of the 58,617 pupils enrolled in 215 schools. The worst affected school had up to 49 per cent of its total school pupil population made up of orphans. Only 6 schools in this district had less than 10 per cent of their enrolled pupils who were orphans. Table 2 gives a breakdown of schools' population by divisions (a division is an administrative unit within a district). The most recent statistics show that Tanzania had a cumulative total of 730,000 AIDS orphans by the end of 1997 (UNICEF, 1999).

On average, more than 25 per cent of the schools' population in the district are orphans. This figure is extremely high and school processes may need to take account of the orphans' concerns. Secondly, the percentage of orphans suggests that the problem is very similar throughout the district. The situation of orphans in different regions is rather different from one to another (NACP, 1997). It is, for example, indicated that in two Coast and Rukwa regions where data were available, the number of orphans constituted about 11 and 9 per cent of the total children below 18 years of age. In the rest of the regions, systematically collected data on orphans are still missing and/or inaccessible.

Table 2. Primary school pupils' enrolment in Bukoba Rural District, 1995

Division	Number of orphans	Total enrolment	% of orphans
Bugabo	2019	6053	33.7
Katerero	3976	15011	26.5
Kiziba	4162	13060	31.7
Kyamtwara	1637	6168	26.4
Misenye	2450	9974	25.4
Rubale	1931	8351	22.7
Total	16175	58617	27.6

Source: Bukoba District Council Education Office (1996), Monitoring and Evaluation Report for School Year 1994/95

Impact on School Enrolment and Attendance

The increasing number of orphans has affected school enrolment. In one region, enrolment was found to be lower in households where an adult death had occurred in the past 12 months than in households that had not experienced death during the same period (World Bank, 1997). Surnra (1995) attributed low enrolment rates in Kagera region to the recent effect of AIDS, saying that 'as more and more children suffer the trauma of being orphans', school enrolment suffered. In his regional ranking of school enrolment of children aged 7–13, he shows that Kagera, once one of the leading regions in terms of pupil enrolment in the country, came last out of 20 Tanzanian mainland regions. Only 44 per cent of 7–13 year olds in the region were enrolled in school. Some of the reasons for this include children's involvement in household activities and the inability of fostering families to send them to school. It has been noted that children in the Kagera region who had lost their mother spent more time on domestic chores than children in other categories (also see Ainsworth, 1993; World Bank, 1997). It was also noted that in households where a female death had occurred, children spent more time on domestic chores than in households that had not experienced any death, since the family's labour force was reduced following a death and the effect of a prolonged period of care.

According to Sumra (1995), AIDS has contributed to low enrolment and poor school attendance in afflicted communities (also see World Bank, 1997; MOEC-URT, 1995). Some of the fostering families do not care about sending fostered children to school. It should be noted here that the importance of sending and keeping the child in school depends very much on the value attached to the individual child's education by the foster household members. As observed by Ainsworth (1993):

> . . . *lower enrolment among paternal orphans in the long run may be explained by other male adults in the household not seeing children in the same manner as a father would.*

This view is in agreement with the conclusions of Foster et al. (1995), who found that maternal rather than paternal families tended to be more concerned and involved with the welfare of the orphans. Grandparents are often responsible for fostering many children. They tend, however, to be less energetic in school matters due to both old age and their generally poorer economic position (Barnett and Blaikie, 1992; Ainsworth, 1993; Foster et al., 1995, 1996; Norman, 1996; Webb, 1997; World Bank, 1997). Foster et al. (1996) noted that orphans in grandparents' homes are likely to experience 'poor feeding practices and health seeking behaviour . . . due to reduced abilities to earn money and produce food'.

The General Impact of AIDS on the Family

The evidence from the discussions indicated that the community has already realised that orphanhood is growing much faster than the capacity of the society to support orphaned children. It was conceded that support of orphaned children can be managed for the first few days after death but declines with time as the fostering households face the day-to-day realities of life with increased costs of care and education (see also Hunter et al., 1997; Shaeffer, 1993).

The impact of AIDS can be classified into three categories: impact on the labour force; impact on household cash flows due to expenditure and high medical costs; and impact on health, nutrition and household food security (Tibaijuka, 1997; World Bank, 1997; Barnett and Blaikie, 1992).

Impact on the Household and Community Labour-force

At household level, the labour loss is partly due to the time a patient spends in bed before his/her ultimate death and the amount of time the caregivers spend with him/her. The discussion with teachers and community members only approximated the AIDS patient's bedridden time to be longer than 5 months. Tibaijuka puts the time at about 6 months. The duration of sickness ranges from three to 9 months and about 7 days are spent on mourning by the members of the family. This time, plus that of admissions in hospital, adds up to the total diverted time from economic activities by the victim's family. The AIDS deaths were estimated to account for 56 per cent of overall mortality in the area.

Thus, the impact on individual families is determined by the number of deaths in the immediate family and in the community plus the time spent on nursing the sick. If the patient is the head of the family, nursing is intensified both in terms of financial expenditure and emotional care. It was reported that involvement of every member of the family had severe implications on the labour force. According to Tibaijuka, the 'aggregated labour stocks in labour/man-equivalents dropped a full 38 per cent and as much as 83 per cent in one household which had to close down and the orphans absorbed into the households of relatives'. This deprives the victim's family of a great deal of time for food production and other economic activities. Children are not spared from this family duty of caring for the sick (Mukoyogo and Williams, 1990).

At village level, community members expend time on mourning and pay frequent visits to HIV/AIDS patients. According to tradition, attendance at funerals is compulsory for every community member and defaulters are ostracised. The practice halts all intensive farming activities to allow mourning for the dead. This amounts to significant loss of production time and the amount of man-hours lost can be calculated by multiplying the number of days allowable by the number of burials in that community (Nindi, 1991; Tibaijuka, 1997). The economic pressure arising from funerals and nursing the sick has forced some changes in the number of mourning days from seven to three and there is now greater leniency for those who work soon after burial (Tibaijuka, 1997; Kinyanjui and Katabaro, 1993).

Impact on Household Cash Flow

In one study area, the average cost of nursing and funeral was averaged to Tsh35,000, that is Tsh200 per day in the six-month period when the AIDS patient was bedridden. The range is quoted to be Tsh16,000–135,000 depending on the family's economic position. This average expenditure equates to about 64 per cent of the average total per capita income (family cash income and subsistence) of Tsh55,000, using Tibaijuka's estimate in the area and 96 per cent of the average household cash income of about Tsh36,000 per annum. In many victim's families this has led to massive borrowing and/or sale of family properties, including farm land and live-stock (Tibaijuka, 1997). In this area, for example, Tibaijuka provides cases where property had been sold to cover medical costs:

Out of the 18 incidences only five reported using their own family savings. Among the rest funds were either borrowed or assets sold including: land (four cases); some cattle (two cases); all cattle (two cases); goats (two cases); bicycle (one case); radio (one case); and [one bunch of] bananas (all cases). Two households reported to have sold all their cattle while one sold half of their banana coffee plot.

In many average families there are the additional costs of school fees and other school needs for the children. This suggests, and it has been observed to be true (Mukoyogo and Williams, 1990), that the remaining orphaned children find it difficult to cope in a poverty-stricken family where all resources were directed to medical attention. The only option for such children is to drop out of school.

Impact on Household Health, Nutrition and Food Security
Health, nutrition and house food supply is yet another form of the impact that families face as a result of AIDS. Tibaijuka (1997) argues that in the case study area the dependency ratio, i.e. the actual number of people involved in production as against the number of all consumers in a household changed, suggesting that the dependency burden increased in some households by 34 per cent, while in others the figure doubled. These changes meant that the surviving members (the elderly and orphans) would have more difficult times than before the AIDS deaths. Along with these burdens go the changes in food supply which deteriorates as a result of reallocation of production time to nursing and care for the sick. It has been reported that deterioration of food supply in many households was attributed to lack of labour due to the fact that the large part of food supply is grown in the family's farm, depending on the labour of family members.

The Impact of AIDS at National Level
The assessment of the impact of AIDS at the national level is rather difficult, particularly in the developing countries where many people live in

absolute poverty. The most direct ones are those observed in drop-outs from school and/or failure to enrol in school due to the financial constraints of their fostering families (Tibaijuka, 1997). Another impact has been the capacity of the medical services to deal with other diseases. In Tanzania, it is estimated that AIDS patients in hospitals account for more than 40 per cent of hospital beds and that they consume (and will continue to do so) the most essential drugs that would be used to treat people with curable diseases (ParProSo, 1994). This condition is particularly threatening as the Tanzanian health system is already overstretched.

The net effect of the impact of AIDS may be visible in a broader sense of economic development of the country. Children are increasingly withdrawing from school to engage in the labour market. This premature engagement has implications for long-term human capital investment, and hence will have adverse effects on other areas of the economy such as reduced production in other sectors. The immediate visible effect, however, is the general deterioration of the family's living standard as shown by Tibaijuka (1997). There is no doubt that such family situations pose a great threat to the provision of education.

Coping with HIV/AIDS

The AIDS Education Programme as a Coping Strategy

The AIDS education programme in Tanzania, as elsewhere, has an overall objective of reversing the current trend of the further spread of HIV infection and AIDS. As a strategy, the programme aims to change behaviour and offers coping skills to those who have already been affected (people who are HIV-positive, their relatives and other members of society). The implementation of this programme is being carried out by a number of NGOs and government departments. It should be noted here that many NGOs operate with different strategies and in different places. The diversity of places where these NGOs are operating and different strategies used has a bearing on the end results of the programmes. This is particularly so where NGOs have different perceptions of the problem (for example, when they are influenced by religious beliefs). The use of condoms among young people and in primary schools has led to many problems in the fight against the epidemic.

On the methods used, the study found that different NGOs have adopted various methods but the common ones include seminars, campaigns, rallies, peer education counselling, church teachings, posters and leaflets for the general population. In schools, classroom instruction is used alongside guest speakers, who include health workers/educators from some of the organisations based in the area. A discussion method among pupils was adopted, rather than a teacher-dominated one, to encourage pupils to talk about AIDS. This has, however, been criticised by some teachers for ineffectiveness because of limited participation by all pupils. It is argued that girls' participation was very low as they could not ask questions or contribute to the discussion except where teachers directed questions to them for 'yes' and 'no' responses. It should be noted here that this method may not be the best for such sensitive social subjects. It is also possible that there are still some influences of the traditional methods in teaching this subject where students remain passive listeners. Peer education is becoming popular as a means to communicate AIDS education messages, both in schools and to the rest of the community. The effectiveness of these methods may vary depending on people's perceptions and attitudes, socio-cultural factors and the key actors in the programme.

Positive Impact of the Programme

It is clear from the findings that people have changed their attitudes towards AIDS victims and their respective family members. Practical aspects relating to sexual activities have also changed with people becoming, or claiming to be, faithful to their sexual partners or wives/husbands. Knowledge and awareness about HIV/AIDS was seen to be high, especially on the modes of transmission and preventive methods. There is a high demand for condoms, and education on how to use condoms (even in schools, where it was not expected). Response to counselling services was also reported to be high. All these were attributed to AIDS education. Thus, no doubt, it has made a positive impact.

Negative Impact of the Programme

Although the community was described as positive as regards AIDS education in the schools in general and for children in particular, there were reservations among parents that AIDS education contradicts some cultural values. For example, boys and girls were not expected to discuss together matters pertaining to sex. This is true of the situation where teachers of either sex are expected to talk about sex with pupils of a different sex. Parents' acceptance of some sex-related issues being discussed in schools or between boys and girls should not be taken for granted or pushed too far (Lwihula, 1988).

It also appeared that collective community efforts to fight the pandemic were suppressed by the presence of external agencies in the form of NGOs. Most of the NGOs have entered the communities with ready-made packages for arresting community problems related to HIV/AIDS. In the process, this has created dependency among community members. The communities think that the solutions lie with the NGOs. As a result, the traditional institutions are no longer operating.

On the school system, AIDS education has added more aspects to consider before any decision is taken. By and large, the addition of another subject becomes a burden on already overloaded timetables and teachers. For example, the majority of teachers interviewed pointed out that the teaching of AIDS education was another burden on them. Secondly, the time allocated to AIDS education (40 minutes a week) was not adequate given the content and teaching method advised. These two factors were considered to compromise the effective teaching of the traditional subjects.

It was suggested by some teachers interviewed that teacher training was inadequate, both in terms of quality and quantity (see also Nyirenda). For example, the training of teachers on AIDS lasted for 5 days and only three teachers attended from each school. One wonders whether 5 days can be sufficient time to re-orient teachers to a new subject and its methods of teaching. It should be noted here that inappropriate training could lead to ineffective results which may turn out to be disastrous.

In the light of the above-mentioned negative impacts of the programme, a question mark against the sustainability of the programme emerges. It is that the AIDS programme cannot be sustained by the people themselves.

Effectiveness of AIDS Education: Are Schoolchildren Coping?

School pupils' perceptions of AIDS as a problem were also investigated. The majority of pupils' responses indicated that AIDS caused a lot of problems to the community and the nation at large. The high death rate was mentioned as one of the problems; this also reduced the work force, affecting the economic development of the country. Loss of weight and vulnerability to long-established illnesses were also pointed out as effects of AIDS. Some pupils (less than 15 per cent) pointed out family separation, lack of parental care and negative attitudes towards work as other effects of AIDS in the community. Some pupils mentioned problems facing their friends who have lost their parents and have consequently been forced to abandon school for lack of school equipment.

Methodological problems arise in assessing how school pupils cope with HIV/AIDS. This is partly because most of these pupils are just on the receiving end: they receive orders to go to school and/or to leave school to look for school contributions. The statements below, however, show a greater awareness of pupils and how they handle some of the problems they face.

I have benefited because I now know that kissing and hugging a person can not transmit HIV. We were misinformed that kissing could transmit the HIV virus.

Another pupil had this to say:

It has helped me to know that AIDS disease is not a God-given disease. If you change your behaviour you can't get the disease. I now know the modes of transmission and those which are not.

Another pupil added:

AIDS education through peer-education has enabled us to pass over the AIDS messages to other people. Whoever is exposed to AIDS education has a role to convey the message to other people as well.

It is now clear to me that kissing and engaging in sexual activities causes AIDS. I also know that eating with an AIDS patient does not cause AIDS and I have learnt how to handle AIDS patients and love them.

On the part of teachers, it was clear from the interviews that greater awareness of AIDS had been achieved as exemplified by the statements below.

Some pupils in standards V–VII already knew about condoms and probably their uses. These are mature pupils. Some are above 17 years old. For some of our girls, there is no doubt of their involvement in premarital sex. Pregnancies and abortions have been reported here. We need to help them.

They argued that some pupils were already aware of and practised sex.

It is wrong if we pretend they are not involved is sexual affairs. If this is so how do they contract STDs? How do they become pregnant? Let them be taught so that they can play it safely.

I stay in the village where most of the pupils come from. I have my brother's and sister's sons and daughters. How can I teach them about condoms? How do I demonstrate it? It is not realistic!

Another female teacher, upset by her colleagues who favoured teaching about condoms, said:

How can a female teacher talk or do anything about condoms before the students? Where will you pass and where will you live? It sounds awkward for a woman to talk about these things in public and especially before the pupils.

It can be concluded that although school pupils and the community at large have benefited from AIDS education, there are still problems relating to the programme which mean that it needs to be modified to take cultural factors into account.

Community Coping Strategies: The Orphan Problem

Any assessment of how people cope with HIV/AIDS is not complete without looking at the issue of orphans and their access to education. The findings of this study reveal elements of imbalance between orphaned and non-orphaned children in terms of care, love and educational support by household members (see also Jallow and Hunt, 1991). It was reported that the educational needs of orphaned children were often disregarded. Whereas there is no dispute about the physical needs of orphaned and non-orphaned children, AIDS-orphaned children may have additional and unique problems as a result of community perceptions of AIDS and the pre-AIDS death social conditions that these children experience. Mann et al. (1992) have noted that:

Children who lose one or both parents to AIDS experience psychological trauma that can be devastating. The experience is not directly analogous to, say, the death of a parent in war or by accident. Instead, children are likely to spend 6 months to several years living with a parent who slowly deteriorates and who has chronic infection . . . (1992:677)

Mwanga (1992) views children who have lost their parents to AIDS as experiencing a different form of bereavement to other causes of death. He observed:

Parental loss through AIDS has created a new form of bereavement. Offspring not only have to deal with parental loss and family disintegration but very often the stigma, fear, guilt and shame the society imposed on AIDS.

'Fear, guilt and shame' were attributed to negative perceptions by the society of the AIDS victim and the stigma experienced by other members of the afflicted family. These problems are magnified further by relatives' feelings about their imminent responsibilities for the children who are left.

It is difficult to make any conclusive generalisation on the differences between AIDS orphans and those orphaned by other causes. However, it is important to note that the development process of children who lose one or both parents is disrupted and that the extent to which this is overcome depends on the creation of a new and hopeful environment. There is evidence suggesting a bleak future for AIDS orphans (Hunter et al., 1997). In recent studies in Tanzania, AIDS-orphaned children have been observed to perform poorly in school-related activities (Katabaro, 1999).

The effects of AIDS on the family, and the increasing number of orphans, brings the smooth functioning of the extended family system into question. In Tanzania, the extended family system is still dominant in many communities. It can be assumed, therefore, that orphaned children are not in danger of being on their own. However, the assumption that this system will cope with the problem of orphans is not guaranteed (World Bank, 1997). The quality of treatment and care, however, depends on the relationship between the orphan and the family members (World Bank, 1997).

The community, too, has a role in determining the child's entitlements within the family. An orphaned girl cannot be expected to gain access to education from her fostering parents when resources are limited (World Bank, 1997; Ainsworth and Over, 1994). Orphaned boys, too, may find it difficult to persuade a nonbiological family to invest in him by providing him with education, for fear that he will move elsewhere on attaining independence. On the other hand, a biological family expects to gain more materially from boys than from girls, whose benefits are seen as short-term. Boys have the advantage of being regarded as future heads of the family and all benefits accruing from investing in them are expected to be enjoyed by the whole family. However, decisions regarding who should and should not have access to education are clearly related to the level of resources in fostering homes (Kongwa et al., 1991; Ross and Reijer, 1995).

Secondly, lack of love and other forms of mistreatment of orphans may be the result of low socio-economic power rather than conscious and deliberate acts against individual orphans. The ailing economy at local and national levels is exacerbating already disintegrating extended family structures which can no longer effectively support orphans (Cross and Whiteside, 1996; Kongwa et al., 1991). Kongwa et al. (1991) noted that:

> *Discrimination is noticed through the failure of the extended family to prioritise the school opportunity and needs for orphans above non-orphans . . . the overstretching of the extended family is demonstrated by the poor feeding and poor status of most orphans.*

It should be emphasised that stigmatisation and/or discrimination against AIDS orphans typically reflects the lack of education on AIDS and its related problems and the economic conditions of the foster families (Kongwa, 1991).

Orphaned children can be supported in the community in different ways.

Bor and Elford (1994) have listed three types of adoption: 'within the family', 'outside the family' and 'orphanage centres'. In countries such as Uganda, Zambia and Zimbabwe, child-headed families are emerging as a distinct family type (Geballe et al., 1995). Such families have been identified in some communities in Tanzania. The next section focuses on the support of orphaned children in Tanzania.

Adoption Within the Extended Family

The study revealed that children are, or can be, adopted or fostered within their own extended family. One or more member(s) of the family networks, voluntarily or from a sense of obligation, take the children into his/her family (usually paternal aunts, uncles, grandparents or other very close relatives). Where this coping mechanism is still functioning, all such children are shared mutually among family members. It is expected that the adopting families will assume all parental responsibilities and, in turn, these children reciprocate through respect and obedience.

Adoption Outside the Extended Family

An alternative adoption or fostering route is where members from outside the extended family come forward to take care of these children, usually when there are no close family members to take them. This type of adoption may arise from the sympathy that community members have towards AIDS-orphaned children. The adopting families are expected to take the same level of responsibility for these children as they would do for their own biological children.

Adoption by Orphanage Centres

Orphanage centres are known to have cared for orphaned children for many years now. More often than not, orphanage centres foster children who cannot be absorbed by family relatives after losing their parents.

These centres are mainly charitable organisations such as religious groups and other NGOs. Their capacity is limited and they can only take a limited number of children in a certain geographical location. It is not clear for how long children can remain in these centres, especially after becoming adults. Children living in centres are assumed to be different from those adopted or fostered in families within the community because of the institutional nature of the centres (see also Durkin, 1995: 103).

The option of integrating orphans into other families is viable but is becoming increasingly impractical. It is very much subject to the existence of families ready to bear an additional burden and the willingness and ability of orphans themselves to accept their new homes. This is particularly difficult for older children who have already established close ties with their parents. Adoption without the child's consent sets back their emotional and social development. In areas of Tanzania, some families' willingness to accept orphans has been inhibited by the belief that the orphans may spread AIDS to other children. This has been a problem in other affected areas where some schools have not wished to admit orphans for fear that they would spread AIDS to other school pupils (see also Barnett and Blaikie, 1992).

The issue of the operating costs of orphanages should not be under-estimated. Ainsworth and Over (1994: 230) have shown that the social cost of institutional care for orphans was too high compared to subsidised homes. The institutional option should handle the immediate problems of orphans, giving the community a chance to initiate community-based programmes in collaboration with government and helping NGOs to strengthen their capacities for sustainability. This is particularly important given the funding of NGOs, the time and space constraints and their objective-specific nature (Preble, 1990; Cross and Whiteside, 1996). It is difficult, for example, for any single NGO to support and care for an orphan from childhood through to adolescence or adulthood. It has been observed that institutional care as a substitute for family care will be limited due to the increasing number of orphans (Barnett and Blaikie, 1992). Cross and Whiteside (1996) feel that, though subsidised, the home option remains unpredictable as a result of inadequate information about attitudes and other home facilities, particularly in relation to educational support and social services.

Many of the programmes initiated by government and NGOs have adopted a system of supporting selected bereaved and AIDS-afflicted families on the assumption that these families cannot cope with the AIDS situation alone. There are good reasons to support these assumptions, but the family's contribution to its own maintenance is of vital importance for the success of sustainable programmes.

Non-adopted Cases

The last category of children are those who for some reason may not be adopted or fostered at all. This group of children falls into two sub-categories: the first is a 'child-headed' family which leads its own life in the parents' homestead under the guidance of the older child. The children may be (and usually are) supervised, albeit informally, by their adult neighbours. Being a new form of family very little is known how this functions. The second sub-category is 'street children' who migrate to urban areas. These are children of no fixed abode who more often than not engage in undesirable behaviour such as theft, smoking and alcoholism. The majority of these children would have dropped out of school, if they had been admitted before.

Problems Facing Orphans

The study revealed a number of problems facing orphans. These problems include discrimination, stigma and ostracism against individuals and families afflicted by AIDS, with orphans suffering most. It is argued that,

71

in addition to their loss of education and other social services:

'Children who lose a parent to AIDS suffer grief and confusion like any other orphan. However, their loss is often worsened by prejudice and social exclusion, and can lead to the loss of education, health care, and the loss of property they may be entitled to inherit should the second parent die as well. The resulting poverty and isolation can create a vicious circle' (UNAIDS, 1997)

These problems have been observed elsewhere with illustrations of the nature and cause of psycho-social problems among orphaned children (Mukoyogo and Williams, 1991; Ngowi and Hogan, 1992). The WHO/ UNICEF report (1994) identified some of the possible sources of psycho-social problems among orphaned children as:

- witnessing the slow, miserable death of one, and possibly both, parents;

- often the subsequent loss of their siblings, their home and property, their friends, school – in fact everything that until then has made up their world;

- a move to an unfamiliar home and pattern of life, with little or no choice in the matter;

- school teachers unsympathetic to their difficulties and often too ready to punish them for being late or ill-equipped, without looking for explanations;

- experiencing relatives haggling over the division of their dead parents' property, sometimes immediately after the funeral;

- multiple loss, first of parents and then of the care givers who had taken them in;

- the prospects for some of them having to fend for themselves if their parents die; anxiety about abuse from adults, mostly relatives, and about having to drop out of school.

Soon after the loss of parent(s), orphans are more vulnerable to psychological problems, such as depression, withdrawal and low self-esteem. Such feelings have long-term effects on child development and active participation in society (Ngowi and Hogan, 1992; Mukoyogo and Williams, 1991). Ngowi and Hogan (1992) have associated the family's intactness with a type of resultant psychopathology. They argue that a disrupted or dysfunctional family stands a greater chance of evolving a pathology that resembled psychosis. This may cause serious problems in the development of orphaned children. Mwanga (1992) has noted that orphans are sometimes difficult to care for by their foster parents because they display antisocial behaviour due to their underlying feelings of anger and resentment. Social and emotional conditions of orphaned children become worse (Sengendo and Nambi, 1997) upon losing their parents. They may, for example, fail to develop positive attitudes and relationships with other members in the community (Ngowi and Hogan, 1992).

The findings of the current study can be illustrated well by one systematic study in Tanzania, in which two children were studied. The study indicated the complexity surrounding orphanhood and bereavement and the shortcomings in dealing with such problems (Ngowi and Hogan, 1992). Both teachers and carers seem not to be well-equipped to detect problems facing the orphaned children and, therefore, should not be expected to help such children. Thus we should not be over-ambitious in believing that adoption and/or fostering of orphans will always result in orphans' quick adjustment, coping or better lives in their new families.

In short, the problems facing orphaned children fall into two broad categories. First, there are problems that emanate from the socio-economic conditions of the society at large and the fostering households in particular – or poverty. In some households, the provision of essential needs is problematic and orphans may be put at the end of the queue for such needs. In many instances, orphans have to work for a living. Other fostering households are not capable of sending to and/or retaining these children in school. Government and the community's immediate support is in many cases lacking. These conditions lead to the second category of psycho-social problems. Because of the inadequacy of resources, orphans do not receive the same treatment as the parents' biological children. This may have negative effects on their emotional and self-concept development, especially because of the way AIDS is perceived in the community. The high number of orphaned children and the general poverty in Tanzania have tremendously affected the extended family structure. This has several implications on the role and functions of the family in relation to the provision of social services such as education and child care.

How is the Tanzanian Government Coping?

Tanzania's Education and Training policy acknowledges that orphaned children constitute a group of 'minority' children in the provision of education (MOEC-URT, 1995). In the light of Tanzania's commitment to provide primary education to all school-age children, the government is committed to giving special attention to these marginal groups as noted in its formal educational policy (MOEC-URT, 1995: 25).

The official school entry age in Tanzania is 7 years. However, some pupils are admitted well beyond this age. In the 1998 school year, only 74 per cent of total primary school enrolment was in the expected age group (7–13) for this level (MOECURT, 1999). Admission into any level of education depends on the capability of the (fostering) parents to meet the cost of education. This is irrespective of the government policy that 'primary education shall be universal and compulsory to all children at the age of seven years until they complete this cycle of education . . . [and] shall continue to be of seven years duration and compulsory in enrolment and attendance' (MOECURT, 1995). There is evidence to show low enrolment at primary school level (Galabawa, 1994; Sunira 1995;

Cooksey et al., 1991) and some of the reasons advanced are the lack of the family's financial capability and the different effects of AIDS (Sumra, 1995). The cost of education at primary school level has meant that pupils are required to pay what is popularly referred to as a 'Universal primary education' (UPE) contribution of about Tsh. 2000/– (equivalent to GM 2.00) per annum. There are also other contributions intended to help with the maintenance and expansion of the school plant and the procurement of equipment such as desks and teaching/learning materials. In addition, contributions ranging from Tsh. 1,000.00–5,000.00 (GB£1.00 to £5.00) can be instituted when deemed necessary by the school bodies and educational authorities. In addition to school contributions, parents are required to buy exercise books, pens, school uniforms and text books as government supply of text books is limited to a few copies only. Over and above these costs, parents face other maintenance costs for health, food and clothing.

Household support for education entails provision of essential learning materials and payment of necessary financial contributions as determined by the relevant authorities. The pupil's family is expected to meet the cost of education of their child(ren) if sponsorship from respective govermnents was not available to them (Komba, 1994). On average, each pupil is expected to have at least 22 exercise books to cover all the subjects. The govermnent's increasing withdrawal from its responsibility to provide schools with textbooks and other school materials, means that pupils' respective families have to buy textbooks as well. Their ability to do this is, however, limited because of the financial constraints individual families are facing. Furthermore, families are expected to pay school fees as indicated before.

The near certainty that more children will be orphaned due to AIDS in developing countries (WHO/GPA, 1995) and the prospect that traditional coping mechanisms to support orphans are now on the verge of collapse, means it is time to re-examine critically the situation of AIDS in these communities. Although various support programmes in affected areas have been initiated, the traditional coping mechanism of incorporating children into the extended family remains the most viable option as a base for community life and has to be supported by informed decisions. Different categories of orphans in need of care and support may require specialised forms of skills and support services which are still lacking. Street children, for example, will demand different levels of attention from those who have been adopted within their extended families or are in orphanage centres. At present, the distribution of support is unclear: patterns of adoption must be clarified if further external support and meaningful intervention in essential services, such as education, are to succeed.

The absence of a clear government policy regarding the school attendance of orphaned children, their payment of fees and other school requirements has several practical implications. There is need to review some of the regulations that guide the provision of primary education in order to ensure equal access for all children. The review of school sessions from a double to a single session per day is a timely coping strategy to many related problems. This change will allow pupils to help their (foster) parents in domestic chores. There is a great need for AIDS-affected governments to ensure clear policies which allow orphaned children to have access to free education through practical solutions. Platform solutions will continue to pull the poor victims of HIV/AIDS from school instead of offering them chances to receive a tool that would liberate them from misery.

4. Summary Conclusions

The overall purpose of these case studies was to assess the impact of HIV/ AIDS on education in the selected districts of Kenya and Tanzania and the various mechanisms in place in the affected communities to address the impact and challenges in education.

The study approach adopted was a case study of Bondo District and some Nairobi slums in Kenya, while in Tanzania the study was conducted in Bukoba and Muleba districts in the northwest of the country, on the shores of Lake Victoria. The case study approach was believed to provide thorough and in-depth information. It arises from the distinctive need to understand the complex social phenomena in the spread and response to the HIV/AIDS pandemic. The case study districts were among the areas with the highest HIV/AIDS infection.

The data collection techniques adopted for the case studies included a documentary review covering a variety of sources ranging from media reports, research reports, workshop and conference reports, teaching materials, circulars, posters and leaflets. There were also focus group discussions, unstructured interviewing schedules, questionnaires and checklists.

A wide range of stakeholders were selected from all the sampled districts, including teachers, NGO staff and education officers, as well as community leaders. A number of government and NGO officers involved in anti-HIV/AIDS programmes at national level were also interviewed.

Data were analysed quantitatively and qualitatively. Qualitative data were computed into means and tabulated for interpretation, while qualitative data were analysed by identifying themes and trends and categorising them for interpretation and analysis.

From the analysis, it is clear that almost everyone in the communities studied has heard about the HIV virus and AIDS, although the problem appears to be one of assessing how widespread the infection is and its overall impact. However, there appears to be some reluctance to admit the severity of HIV/AIDS; the general tendency of many people in the surveyed communities is not to actualise or admit the seriousness of the HIV/AIDS menace. They perceive it as a common problem in their day-to-day lives which has taken its toll among children, the young people and the middle-aged as well as the old. Some people still believe that HIV/AIDS is someone's creation and that its treatment is being deliberately withheld to extensively reduce their populations.

On the basis of the research method adopted by the case studies, determining the mortality rate with sufficient supportive evidence was quite difficult. This was partly due to lack of concrete information regarding HIV/AIDS cases because of lack of openness about the menace. It was also difficult to verify mortality rates with the local district hospital records. It appeared from the FGDs and interviews, however, that mortality rates of HIV/AIDS-related cases are high. Children have been infected at birth and have therefore not lived long enough to attend school. There are some cases of children being enrolled in school only to drop out in order to earn money to support their families and help with health care expenses for their ill relatives.

At the national level, especially in Kenya, there is some evidence of increased mortality as reflected in the recent national census, the overall results of which showed a national decrease in the projected population. The case studies also revealed that the HIV/AIDS pandemic seems to be the most single important health challenge that Kenya and Tanzania, as indeed other parts of the developing countries, are facing. It is the major health problem and has the potential to reverse the significant gains made in recent years in life expectancy and infant mortality.

The disease was said to be transmitted in various ways including the sharing of sharp instruments such as needles during injections or piercing ears, attending to HIV/AIDS patients, especially through washing their bodies which have sores, as well as negligence in blood transfusion. However, unprotected sexual intercourse was identified as the major cause.

The overall goal of the governments of Kenya and Tanzania is to slow down the progression of the HIV/AIDS epidemic, eventually bringing it to a halt, and to adequately respond to the consequences of the epidemic. To realise such goals, the governments have solicited funds from bilateral and multilateral donors and have increased their own funding. HIV/AIDS programmes have been launched which have focused on aspects such as management, information, education and communication, clinical services, counselling and mitigation of socio-economic impacts, epidemiology, surveillance, research and blood testing.

Although the programmes reflect a genuine effort to combat the spread of the pandemic, the response in the two countries was slow and took root after the disease had had far-reaching devastating effects. Generally, the programmes have not worked synergetically with most of them being sporadic and patchy. Lack of political will in combating the pandemic is manifest at all levels of the political leadership, especially in Kenya.

To cope with HIV/AIDS at the community level, it was noted that there have been intensive sensitisation campaigns especially in the urban areas to warn the public about the HIV/AIDS problem. This has been done through public meetings convened by local leaders, churches which give warnings about the dangers of the disease as well as providing counselling services. Hospitals and clinics use antenatal visits to expose mothers to the dangers of the pandemic. On the whole, the sensitisation campaigns appear effective among the adult populations although more still has to be done to change people's attitudes and behaviour.

Households use a variety of strategies to cope with the economic shock of a prime-age adult death. The most commonly applied strategy is drawing on family savings or selling assets. The ownership of land, livestock, bicycles and radios is quite widespread in the rural areas. Many households that suffer an adult's death do sell some of their durable goods as part of their coping strategy.

The death of a parent or another adult in the household quite often affects the nutritional status of surviving children by reducing household income and food expenditure. Such nutritional reduction impedes intellectual development and a person's long-run productivity. The effects of a prime-age death also decrease enrolment in school among children in the household due to the reduction in the ability of families to pay for schooling and raising the demand for children's labour. Children are withdrawn from school to work outside the home, help with chores and farming, or care for an ailing family member.

It is clear that the communities studied are experiencing tremendous social strain in their attempt to cope with large numbers of HIV/AIDS orphans. At the family level there is already an increased burden and stress on extended family structures. Many grandparents and relatives are caring for young children and many go without basic amenities. Many of the problems they experience at the household and community levels contribute to considerable school absenteeism and drop-out rates.

At the school level, it is clear from the case studies that pupils are well aware of the causes and dangers of HIV/AIDS. They learn of the problem from a variety of sources which include the media and school. The HIV/AIDS education programme, especially in Kenya, appears quite weak. Despite the lack of a formalised approach in teaching about HIV/AIDS, schools in different regions have attempted various ways of imparting AIDS education including specific programmes, poems and drama tailored towards the disease.

Schools also try to cope with HIV/AIDS through material support for those affected especially in cases of deaths, through contributions to funerals by way of donations and the provision of labour.

AIDS orphans generally have problems coping with the numerous school levies, which in the end exclude them from school participation, although some of the schools give a special remission to such children. In the urban areas, there is a growing phenomenon of rehabilitation centres for children in need of special protection, such as HIV/AIDS orphans.

HIV/AIDS has an obvious effect on the management of teachers, especially their personal interactions with their peers, pupils and job retention. Many sick teachers, especially in the rural areas, take hardly any official leave as they fear rumours of stigmatisation and problems of redeployment or replacement. Consequently, some schools are generally understaffed due to problems of sick teachers. The absenteeism of sick teachers is an important contributory factor to overcrowding in many schools.

5. References

Faye, A. (1994). *AIDS Peer Education Training of the Secondary High School Students*, unpublished, Médecins Du Monde, Bukoba.

Gachuhi, D. (1999). *The Impact of HIV/AIDS on Education Systems in the Eastern and Southern African Region and the Response of Education Systems to HIV/AIDS: Life Skills Programmes*. Paper prepared for UNICEF presentation at the All Sub-Saharan Africa Conference on Education for All, December 6–10, 1999, Johannesburg, South Africa.

Government of Kenya and UNICEF (1998). *Situation Analysis of Children and Women in Kenya*. Nairobi: UNICEF Kenya Country Office.

Grout, R.E. (1953). *Health Teaching in Schools*, W.B. Saunders Company, London.

Kaijage, F.J. (1993). 'AIDS Control and the Burden of History in Northern Tanzania in Population and Environment', *Journal of Interdisciplinary Studies* Vol. 14, No. 3.

Katabaro, L.K. (1999). 'School Performance and Perceptions of "AIDS" Orphaned Primary School Pupils: A Case Study of Bukoba District in Tanzania'. A Ph.D. thesis submitted to the University of Cambridge.

Katabaro, J.K. (1993). *The Impact of AIDS on Education in Tanzania: A Case of Bujunangoma Community in Bukoba Rural District, Kagera Region*. Draft manuscript, IDRC Nairobi.

Katabaro, L.K. (1996). *The Impact of Health Education on People's Behaviour and Practice: A Case of Selected Areas in Kagera Region, Tanzania*. Kenya, Uganda and Tanzania Research Awards (KUTERA). Nairobi: International Development Research Centre (IDRC).

Katahoire, A. (1993). *The Impact of AIDS on Education in Uganda: A Case Study of Lyantonde Community*. Draft Manuscript. Nairobi: IDRC.

Killewo, J., (ed) (1992). 'Behavioural and Epidemiological Aspects of AIDS Research in Tanzania'. Proceedings from a Workshop held in Dar-es-Salaam, Tanzania, 6–8 December, 1989. SAREC Documentation.

Klouda, A. (1994). 'Investing in the Future: A Summary of the Review of Global

Policies for the Prevention and Control of HIV.' Work Commissioned by HIV/STD Advisory Centre for ODA.

Levine, R., Obonyo, B.,Malangalila, E., and Mallya, A. (1994). 'Health Financing Alternatives and Legal and Regulatory Analysis for Health'. Working Paper for Investing in Human Capital Workshop, 15–20 April, Arusha, Tanzania.

Lwihula, G. K. (1988). 'Social Cultural Factors Associated with the Transmission of HIV Virus in Tanzania: The Kagera Experience'. A paper presented at the Workshop on Counselling of AIDS Patients at Sokoine University of Agriculture, Morogoro, 30 October–4 November 1988.

Lwihula, G. K. (1989). *Knowledge, Attitudes and Beliefs on AIDS Disease Among Secondary School Students in Kagera Region.*

Lwihula, G. K. (1990). 'Sexual Practices and Patterns of Interaction in the Kagera Area with Reference to the Spread of HIV'. Paper presented at the Seminar on Anthropological Studies Relevant to Sexual Transmission of HIV, Sandberg Centre, Sandborg, Denmark.

MDEC (1990). Kampeni ya Elimu Dhidi ya Ukimwi: Kiongozi cha Mwalimu, Dsm. – Kampeni ya Elimu Dhidi ya Ukimwi: Kitabu cha Mwanafunzi.

MOH-URT (1991). Overview of AIDS Control Activities up to September 1990: Work Plan and Budget, 1 January–31 December 1991.

MOH-URT (1988–93). *National AIDS Control Programme: Surveillance Reports 1–7.*

Muhondwa, E. P. Y., Leshabari, M. T. and Batwa, Y. D. (1991). 'The Joint KA13P/PR Surveys, Preliminary Communication'. Unpublished Survey Report, Dar-es-Salaam.

National AIDS Control Council (2000). *National AIDS Strategy 2000–2005.* Nairobi.

Ndeki, S. S., Klepp, K. I. and Mliga, G. R. (1994). 'Perceived Risk of AIDS and Sexual Behaviour Among Primary School Children in two Areas of Tanzania' in *Health Education Research: Theory and Practice* Vol. 9, No. 1.

Nindi, B. C. (1991). 'Issues in Social Welfare: Adjusting to Regression. Will the Poor Recover?' A paper presented at the 2nd Convocation Seminar, 3–4 April 1991, University of Dar-es-Salaam.

Nyirenda, S.D. (1995). *Review of Implementation of the School AIDS Control Education Programme in Primary Schools in Tanzania*. Report for UNICEF, Tanzania.

Odiwuor, W.H. (2000). *HIV/AIDS and Primary Education in Kenya: Effects and Strategies*. Stockholm: Institute of International Education, University of Stockholm.

Okeyo, T.M. (2000). *National Strategic Plan*. Nairobi.

Republic of Kenya (2000). *Population Census (1999)* Nairobi: Government Printers.

Sawaya, M., Fimbo, V., Mkoba, S. and Owenya, F. (1995). 'Tanzania HIV/AIDS/ STD Education in Schools'. A Country Paper presented at the UNESCO Regional Seminar on AIDS and Education within the School System in Eastern and Southern Africa, Harare, Zimbabwe, 20–24 February, 1995.

Shaeffer, S. (1993). 'Impact of AIDS on Education'. Background paper commissioned by UNESCO, SIDA and IDRC for the 'Experts' Seminar on the Impact of AIDS on Education, IIEP, Paris, 8–10 December, 1993.

Shaeffer, S. (1993). *The UNICEF Perspective on HIV/AIDS*. Bangkok, East Asia and Pacific Office, UNICEF.

Shamseh, P. and Rachel, C. (1991). 'Children Orphaned by AIDS: A call for NGOs and Donors'. Paper presented to the National Council for International Health.

T.R.C.S/DRC (1993). *Explorative Study of Social Support Provided to Orphans in Primary Schools in Bukoba (U & R) Districts: Study Report*.

UNESCO (2000). *The Encounter between HIV/AIDS and Education*. Harare: UNESCO Sub-regional Office for Southern Africa.

WHO (1990). *School Health Education to Prevent AIDS and Sexually Transmitted Diseases*. WHO AIDS Series No. 10. Geneva: World Health Organisation.

WHO/UNESCO (1992). *School Health Education to Prevent AIDS and Sexually Transmitted Diseases*. WHO AIDS Series No 10. Geneva: World Health Organisation.

World Bank (1993). *World Development Report 1993, Investing in Health/World Development Indicators*. Oxford University Press.

World Bank (2000). *Intensifying Action Against HIV/AIDS in Africa: Responding to the Crisis*. Washington: World Bank.